ON WRITING WELL

Books by William Zinsser

Any Old Place with You

Seen Any Good Movies Lately?

The City Dwellers

Weekend Guests

The Haircurl Papers

Pop Goes America

The Paradise Bit

The Lunacy Boom

On Writing Well

Writing with a Word Processor

Willie and Dwike

WILLIAM ZINSSER

ON WRITING WELL

AN INFORMAL GUIDE
TO WRITING NONFICTION

THIRD EDITION
REVISED AND ENLARGED

1817

HARPER & ROW, PUBLISHERS, New York

Cambridge, Philadelphia, San Francisco, London
Mexico City, São Paulo, Singapore, Sydney

Library of Congress Cataloging in Publication Data

Zinsser, William Knowlton.
    On writing well.

Includes bibliographical references and index.
    1. English language—Rhetoric.   2. Exposition
(Rhetoric)   3. Prose literature—Technique.   I. Title.
PE1429.Z5   1985   808'.042   84-48208
ISBN 0-06-015409-8
ISBN (pbk.) 0-06-047397-5

Contents

Preface to the Third Edition

This book, which grew out of a course in writing nonfiction that I originated and taught at Yale, was first published in 1976. Four years later it was expanded to cover a number of subjects that I hadn't thought of including earlier, like professional and business writing, and to keep pace with various changes in the language and the culture.

Now five more years have passed and another 25 percent has been added. As a believer in brevity I deplore such growth: breaking the 200-page barrier is against my principles. But I'm consoled by two thoughts. One is that it's still a small book—its weight won't cause internal injuries to anyone reading it in bed. The other is that I've learned a lot since the Second Edition that has helped me in my own writing and that I think will help other writers, editors and teachers.

Most obviously, the word processor has come along and changed my life. Writers have suddenly been given a miraculous tool that enables them to tinker with their work on a screen until they get it right—in short, to rewrite painlessly and even with enjoyment. Rewriting is the essence of writing, as this book has always insisted. But nowhere in its pages was there an explanation of how to approach the job: what a writer should look for when he revisits his first draft. Chapter 20 is a new chapter that tries to fill in these gaps. On one level it's a beginner's guide to the word processor—

an attempt to take the fear out of the machine and to describe how it helps writers to write well. But inevitably it's also a chapter about rewriting, and anyone looking for advice on that subject will find it here.

Another thing I learned—a lesson that took me by surprise during a writing project of my own—is that truth needs no adornment. Somehow I always thought that a writer had to help his material along by explaining its point or adding his opinion. Then I discovered that readers will bring to a piece of writing all the emotion that a writer could ask for—if he will just get out of the way. The principle strikes me as an important one. I call it "Trust Your Material," and that's what I also call the new chapter (Chapter 21) that describes how I stumbled onto it.

The emphasis of this book has always been on the craft of writing. Too little has been said about attitudes: the attitude that a writer takes toward language and the attitude that he takes toward his work. I have strong opinions on this subject and should have expressed them long ago. Now I have.

First, at the end of Chapter 14 ("Bits & Pieces") I've written five new entries—"The Quickest Fix," "Breeziness," "Taste," "Imitation" and "Eloquence and the Uses of the Past"—which, if not united, are at least related. Together they suggest that writing is cheapened or elevated by certain factors that lie just beneath the surface of what we write, invisible to the eye. They are matters, finally, of attitude: how willing we are to trust the grandeur of the language, the dignity of the reader, and the heritage that makes us who we are.

Secondly, I've written a new final chapter—very much a personal statement—that sums up the attitudes that have always guided my own writing. The chapter is called "Write as Well as You Can." It states my belief that a writer must set higher standards for himself than anybody else sets for him—and then must defend his writing against everyone who gets between him and the printed page. By "everyone" I mainly mean editors, and the chapter discusses the relationship between writers and editors at its helpful best and at its harmful worst—still another subject that *On Writing Well* has never addressed, though the relationship is the crucial one in any writer's life. Ultimately the chapter is about the attitudes that are at the core of a writer's success: confidence, ego and pride.

Another new chapter is the one called "Nonfiction as the New American Literature" (Chapter 8). This book is grounded in the idea that nonfiction is the place where much of the best writing of the day is being done. Yet many writers and teachers of writing continue to feel vaguely guilty if they prefer it to fiction—nonfiction is the slightly disreputable younger brother in the royal house of literature. No such guilt is necessary. While the keepers of the temple weren't looking, nonfiction crept in and occupied the throne. How this happened— how the shifting currents of American life have made us a fact-minded nation and raised nonfiction to a high art—is the subject of Chapter 8. It puts the book in a larger context that it has long needed.

Throughout, I've made revisions to cut outdated references and to add fresh examples. New material has been added, for instance, to the sections on sexism, interviews, business writing and sports. Some writers have been added who were not along on the previous ride, and some have been dropped. Quite a few additions have been woven into the text where they seemed to fit most naturally. Often they are just a few sentences that amplify an existing point or that answer questions that readers have raised. Over the decade of this book's life I have talked with or heard from thousands of writers and editors and teachers all across America. Their affection for the book has been a nourishment to me, and if this Third Edition is both richer in texture and more personal in tone it's because so many people have put some part of themselves into it.

On Writing Well is a highly subjective book—one man's opinions and prejudices. But I've included passages by many other writers to show how they solved a particular problem and to indicate the broad range of possibilities that are open to the nonfiction writer. My purpose is not to teach good nonfiction, or good journalism, but to teach good English that can be put to those uses. Don't assume that bad English can still be good journalism; it can't. All the writers quoted in this book were chosen because they write good English, no matter how "popular" the journal that they originally wrote for. They never talk down to the reader. They are true to themselves and to what they want to say and how they want to say it. They are vastly different in style and personality, but all of them have learned the one lesson that must be learned: how to control their material. You can too.

W.Z.

New York
March 1985

PART I

Principles

1. The Transaction

About ten years ago a school in Connecticut held "a day devoted to the arts," and I was asked if I would come and talk about writing as a vocation. When I arrived I found that a second speaker had been invited—Dr. Brock (as I'll call him), a surgeon who had recently begun to write and had sold some stories to national magazines. He was going to talk about writing as an avocation. That made us a panel, and we sat down to face a crowd of student newspaper editors, English teachers and parents, all eager to learn the secrets of our glamorous work.

Dr. Brock was dressed in a bright red jacket, looking vaguely Bohemian, as authors are supposed to look, and the first question went to him. What was it like to be a writer?

He said it was tremendous fun. Coming home from an arduous day at the hospital, he would go straight to his yellow pad and write his tensions away. The words just flowed. It was easy.

I then said that writing wasn't easy and it wasn't fun. It was hard and lonely, and the words seldom just flowed.

Next Dr. Brock was asked if it was important to rewrite. Absolutely not, he said. "Let it all hang out," and whatever form the sentences take will reflect the writer at his most natural.

I then said that rewriting is the essence of writing. I pointed out that professional writers rewrite their sentences

repeatedly and then rewrite what they have rewritten. I
mentioned that E. B. White and James Thurber rewrote
their pieces eight or nine times.

"What do you do on days when it isn't going well?" Dr.
Brock was asked. He said he just stopped writing and put
the work aside for a day when it would go better.

I then said that the professional writer must establish a
daily schedule and stick to it. I said that writing is a craft,
not an art, and that the man who runs away from his craft
because he lacks inspiration is fooling himself. He is also
going broke.

"What if you're feeling depressed or unhappy?" a student
asked. "Won't that affect your writing?"

Probably it will, Dr. Brock replied. Go fishing. Take a
walk.

Probably it won't, I said. If your job is to write every day,
you learn to do it like any other job.

A student asked if we found it useful to circulate in the
literary world. Dr. Brock said that he was greatly enjoying
his new life as a man of letters, and he told several lavish
stories of being taken to lunch by his publisher and his agent
at Manhattan restaurants where writers and editors gather. I
said that professional writers are solitary drudges who seldom see other writers.

"Do you put symbolism in your writing?" a student asked
me.

"Not if I can help it," I replied. I have an unbroken record
of missing the deeper meaning in any story, play or movie,
and as for dance and mime, I have never had even a remote
notion of what is being conveyed.

"I *love* symbols!" Dr. Brock exclaimed, and he described
with gusto the joys of weaving them through his work.

So the morning went, and it was a revelation to all of us.
At the end Dr. Brock told me he was enormously interested
in my answers—it had never occurred to him that writing

could be hard. I told him I was just as interested in *his* answers—it had never occurred to me that writing could be
easy. (Maybe I should take up surgery on the side.)

As for the students, anyone might think we left them be-
wildered. But in fact we probably gave them a broader
glimpse of the writing process than if only one of us had
talked. For of course there isn't any "right" way to do such
intensely personal work. There are all kinds of writers and
all kinds of methods, and any method that helps somebody
to say what he wants to say is the right method for him.

Some people write by day, others by night. Some people
need silence, others turn on the radio. Some write by hand,
some by typewriter or word processor, some by talking into
a tape recorder. Some people write their first draft in one
long burst and then revise; others can't write the second paragraph until they have fiddled endlessly with the first.

But all of them are vulnerable and all of them are tense.
They are driven by a compulsion to put some part of themselves on paper, and yet they don't just write what comes
naturally. They sit down to commit an act of literature, and
the self who emerges on paper is a far stiffer person than the
one who sat down. The problem is to find the real man or
woman behind all the tension.

For ultimately the product that any writer has to sell is not
his subject, but who he is. I often find myself reading with
interest about a topic that I never thought would interest
me—some unusual scientific quest, for instance. What holds
me is the enthusiasm of the writer for his field. How was he
drawn into it? What emotional baggage did he bring along?
How did it change his life? It's not necessary to want to
spend a year alone at Walden Pond to become deeply involved with a man who did.

This is the personal transaction that's at the heart of good
nonfiction writing. Out of it come two of the most important
qualities that this book will go in search of: humanity and

warmth. Good writing has an aliveness that keeps the reader reading from one paragraph to the next, and it's not a question of gimmicks to "personalize" the author. It's a question of using the English language in a way that will achieve the greatest strength and the least clutter.

Can such principles be taught? Maybe not. But most of them can be learned.

2. Simplicity

Clutter is the disease of American writing. We are a society strangling in unnecessary words, circular constructions, pompous frills and meaningless jargon.

Who can understand the viscous language of everyday American commerce and enterprise: the business letter, the interoffice memo, the corporation report, the notice from the bank explaining its latest "simplified" statement? What member of an insurance or medical plan can decipher the brochure that tells him what his costs and benefits are? What father or mother can put together a child's toy—on Christmas Eve or any other eve—from the instructions on the box? Our national tendency is to inflate and thereby sound important. The airline pilot who announces that he is presently anticipating experiencing considerable precipitation wouldn't dream of saying that it may rain. The sentence is too simple—there must be something wrong with it.

But the secret of good writing is to strip every sentence to its cleanest components. Every word that serves no function, every long word that could be a short word, every adverb that carries the same meaning that's already in the verb, every passive construction that leaves the reader unsure of who is doing what—these are the thousand and one adulterants that weaken the strength of a sentence. And they usually occur, ironically, in proportion to education and rank.

During the late 1960s the president of a major university

wrote a letter to mollify the alumni after a spell of campus unrest. "You are probably aware," he began, "that we have been experiencing very considerable potentially explosive expressions of dissatisfaction on issues only partially related." He meant that the students had been hassling them about different things. I was far more upset by the president's English than by the students' potentially explosive expressions of dissatisfaction. I would have preferred the presidential approach taken by Franklin D. Roosevelt when he tried to convert into English his own government's memos, such as this blackout order of 1942:

> Such preparations shall be made as will completely obscure all Federal buildings and non-Federal buildings occupied by the Federal government during an air raid for any period of time from visibility by reason of internal or external illumination.

"Tell them," Roosevelt said, "that in buildings where they have to keep the work going to put something across the windows."

Simplify, simplify. Thoreau said it, as we are so often reminded, and no American writer more consistently practiced what he preached. Open *Walden* to any page and you will find a man saying in a plain and orderly way what is on his mind:

> I love to be alone. I never found the companion that was so companionable as solitude. We are for the most part more lonely when we go abroad among men than when we stay in our chambers. A man thinking or working is always alone, let him be where he will. Solitude is not measured by the miles of space that intervene between a man and his fellows. The really diligent student in one of the crowded hives of Cambridge College is as solitary as a dervish in the desert.

* * *

How can the rest of us achieve such enviable freedom from clutter? The answer is to clear our heads of clutter. Clear thinking becomes clear writing: one can't exist without the other. It is impossible for a muddy thinker to write good English. He may get away with it for a paragraph or two, but soon the reader will be lost, and there is no sin so grave, for he will not easily be lured back.

Who is this elusive creature the reader? He is a person with an attention span of about twenty seconds. He is assailed on every side by forces competing for his time: by newspapers and magazines, by television and radio, by his stereo and videocassettes, by his wife and children and pets, by his house and his yard and all the gadgets that he has bought to keep them spruce, and by that most potent of competitors, sleep. The man snoozing in his chair with an unfinished magazine open on his lap is a man who was being given too much unnecessary trouble by the writer.

It won't do to say that the snoozing reader is too dumb or too lazy to keep pace with the train of thought. My sympathies are with him. If the reader is lost, it is generally because the writer has not been careful enough to keep him on the path.

This carelessness can take any number of forms. Perhaps a sentence is so excessively cluttered that the reader, hacking his way through the verbiage, simply doesn't know what it means. Perhaps a sentence has been so shoddily constructed that the reader could read it in any of several ways. Perhaps the writer has switched pronouns in mid-sentence, or has switched tenses, so the reader loses track of who is talking or when the action took place. Perhaps Sentence B is not a logical sequel to Sentence A—the writer, in whose head the connection is clear, has not bothered to provide the missing link. Perhaps the writer has used an important word incorrectly by not taking the trouble to look it up. He may think

is too dumb or too lazy to keep pace with the ~~writer's~~ train
of thought. My sympathies are ~~entirely~~ with him.) ~~He's not~~
~~so dumb.~~ (If the reader is lost, it is generally because the
writer ~~of the article~~ has not been careful enough to keep
him on the ~~proper~~ path.

This carelessness can take any number of ~~different~~ forms.
Perhaps a sentence is so excessively ~~long and~~ cluttered that
the reader, hacking his way through ~~all~~ the verbiage, simply
doesn't know what it ~~the writer~~ means. Perhaps a sentence has
been so shoddily constructed that the reader could read it in
any of several ~~two or three different~~ ways. ~~He thinks he knows what~~
~~the writer is trying to say, but he's not sure.~~ Perhaps the
writer has switched pronouns in mid-sentence, or ~~perhaps he~~
has switched tenses, so the reader loses track of who is
talking ~~to whom~~ or ~~exactly~~ when the action took place. Perhaps Sentence B is not a logical sequel to Sentence A -- the
writer, in whose head the connection is ~~perfectly~~ clear, has
not bothered to provide ~~given enough thought to providing~~ the missing link. Perhaps the writer has used an important word incorrectly by not
taking the trouble to look it up ~~and make sure.~~ He may think
that "sanguine" and "sanguinary" mean the same thing, but)
~~I can assure you that~~ (the difference is a bloody big one ~~to the~~
~~reader.~~ The reader ~~He~~ can only ~~try to~~ infer ~~what~~ (speaking of big differences) what the writer is trying to imply.

Faced with these ~~such a variety of~~ obstacles, the reader
is at first a remarkably tenacious bird. He ~~tends to~~ blames
himself. ~~He~~ obviously missed something, ~~he thinks,~~ and he goes
back over the mystifying sentence, or over the whole paragraph,

piecing it out like an ancient rune, making guesses and moving
on. But he won't do this for long. ~~He will soon run out of
patience.~~ (The writer is making him work too hard ~~→harder
than he should have to work~~— and the reader will look for
~~a writer~~ who is better at his craft.

The writer must therefore constantly ask himself: What am
I trying to say? ~~in this sentence?~~ (Surprisingly often, he
doesn't know.) ~~And~~ Then he must look at what he has ~~just~~
written and ask: Have I said it? Is it clear to someone
~~who is coming upon~~ the subject for the first time? If it's
not, ~~clear,~~ it is because some fuzz has worked its way into the
machinery. The clear writer is a person ~~who is~~ clear-headed
enough to see this stuff for what it is: fuzz.

I don't mean ~~to suggest~~ that some people are born
clear-headed and are therefore natural writers, whereas
~~other people~~ are naturally fuzzy and will ~~therefore~~ never write
well. Thinking clearly is ~~an entirely~~ conscious act that the
writer must ~~keep forcing~~ upon himself, just as if he were
~~starting~~ out on any other ~~kind of~~ project that ~~calls for~~ logic:
adding up a laundry list or doing an algebra problem ~~or playing
chess.~~ Good writing doesn't ~~just~~ come naturally, though most
people obviously think ~~it's as easy as walking.~~ The professional

Two pages of the original final manuscript of this chapter. Although
they look like a first draft, they had already been rewritten and re-
typed—like almost every other page—four or five times. With each
rewrite I try to make what I have written tighter, stronger and more
precise, eliminating every element that is not doing useful work. Then
I go over it once more, reading it aloud, and am always amazed at how
much clutter can still be cut. Today, on a word processor, no such
record of my changes would exist. But the principles of editing are
exactly the same (see Chapter 20).

that "sanguine" and "sanguinary" mean the same thing, but
the difference is a bloody big one. The reader can only infer
(speaking of big differences) what the writer is trying to imply.

Faced with these obstacles, the reader is at first a remarkably tenacious bird. He blames himself—he obviously
missed something, and he goes back over the mystifying
sentence, or over the whole paragraph, piecing it out like an
ancient rune, making guesses and moving on. But he won't
do this for long. The writer is making him work too hard,
and the reader will look for one who is better at his craft.

The writer must therefore constantly ask himself: What
am I trying to say? Surprisingly often, he doesn't know.
Then he must look at what he has written and ask: Have I
said it? Is it clear to someone encountering the subject for
the first time? If it's not, it is because some fuzz has worked
its way into the machinery. The clear writer is a person
clear-headed enough to see this stuff for what it is: fuzz.

I don't mean that some people are born clear-headed and
are therefore natural writers, whereas others are naturally
fuzzy and will never write well. Thinking clearly is a conscious act that the writer must force upon himself, just as if
he were embarking on any other project that requires logic:
adding up a laundry list or doing an algebra problem. Good
writing doesn't come naturally, though most people obviously think it does. The professional writer is forever being
bearded by strangers who say that they'd like to "try a little
writing sometime" when they retire from their real profession. Or they say, "I could write a book about that." I doubt
it.

Writing is hard work. A clear sentence is no accident.
Very few sentences come out right the first time, or even the
third time. Remember this as a consolation in moments of
despair. If you find that writing is hard, it's because it *is*
hard. It's one of the hardest things that people do.

3. Clutter

Fighting clutter is like fighting weeds—the writer is always slightly behind. New varieties sprout overnight, and by noon they are part of American speech. John Dean holds the record. In just one day of testimony on TV during the Watergate hearings he raised the clutter quotient by 400 percent. The next day everyone in America was saying "at this point in time" instead of "now."

Consider all the prepositions that are routinely draped onto verbs that don't need any help. Head up. Free up. Face up to. We no longer head committees. We head them up. We don't face problems anymore. We face up to them when we can free up a few minutes. A small detail, you may say—not worth bothering about. It *is* worth bothering about. The game is won or lost on hundreds of small details. Writing improves in direct ratio to the number of things we can keep out of it that shouldn't be there. "Up" in "free up" shouldn't be there. Can we picture anything being freed *up?* The writer of clean English must examine every word that he puts on paper. He will find a surprising number that don't serve any purpose.

Take the adjective "personal," as in "a personal friend of mine," "his personal feeling" or "her personal physician." It is typical of the words that can be eliminated nine times out of ten. The personal friend has come into the language to distinguish him from the business friend, thereby debasing

13

not only language but friendship. Someone's feeling *is* his
personal feeling—that's what "his" means. As for the personal physician, he is that man summoned to the dressing
room of a stricken actress so that she won't have to be
treated by the impersonal physician assigned to the theater.
Someday I'd like to see him identified as "her doctor." Physicians are physicians, friends are friends. The rest is clutter.

Clutter is the laborious phrase which has pushed out the
short word that means the same thing. These locutions are a
drag on energy and momentum. Even before John Dean
gave us "at this point in time," people had stopped saying
"now." They were saying "at the present time," or "current-
ly," or "presently" (which means "soon"). Yet the idea can
always be expressed by "now" to mean the immediate moment ("Now I can see him"), or by "today" to mean the historical present ("Today prices are high"), or simply by the
verb "to be" ("It is raining"). There is no need to say, "At the
present time we are experiencing precipitation."

Speaking of which, we are experiencing considerable difficulty getting *that* word out of the language now that it has
lumbered in. Even your dentist will ask if you are experiencing any pain. If he were asking one of his own children he
would say, "Does it hurt?" He would, in short, be himself.
By using a more pompous phrase in his professional role he
not only sounds more important; he blunts the painful edge
of truth. It is the language of the airline stewardess demon-
strating the oxygen mask that will drop down if the plane
should somehow run out of air. "In the extremely unlikely
possibility that the aircraft should experience such an even-
tuality," she begins—a phrase so oxygen-depriving in itself
that we are prepared for any disaster, and even gasping
death shall lose its sting. As for her request to "kindly ex-
tinguish all smoking materials," I often wonder what materials are smoking. Maybe she thinks my coat and tie are on
fire.

Clutter is the ponderous euphemism that turns a slum into a depressed socioeconomic area, a salesman into a marketing representative and garbage collectors into waste disposal personnel. In New Canaan, Connecticut, the incinerator is now the "volume reduction unit." I think of Bill Mauldin's cartoon showing two hoboes riding a freight train. One of them says, "I started as a simple bum, but now I'm hard-core unemployed."

Clutter is the official language used by the American corporation—in its news release and its annual report—to hide its mistakes. When a big company recently announced that it was "decentralizing its organizational structure into major profit-centered businesses" and that "corporate staff services will be realigned under two senior vice-presidents" it meant that it had had a lousy year.

Clutter is the language of the interoffice memo ("The trend to mosaic communication is reducing the meaningfulness of concern about whether or not demographic segments differ in their tolerance of periodicity") and the language of computers ("Congruent command paradigms explicitly represent the semantic oppositions in the definitions of the commands to which they refer").

Clutter is the language of the Pentagon throwing dust in the eyes of the populace by calling an invasion a "reinforced protective reaction strike" and by justifying its vast budgets on the need for "credible second-strike capability" and "counterforce deterrence." How can we grasp such vaporous double-talk? As George Orwell pointed out in "Politics and the English Language," an essay written in 1946 but cited frequently during the Vietnam and Cambodia years of Johnson and Nixon, "In our time, political speech and writing are largely the defense of the indefensible. . . . Thus political language has to consist largely of euphemism, question-begging and sheer cloudy vagueness." Orwell's warning that clutter is not just a nuisance but a deadly tool came true in America in the 1960s.

In fact, the art of verbal camouflage reached new heights of invention during General Alexander Haig's tenure as Secretary of State in the Reagan administration. Before Haig nobody had ever thought of saying "at this juncture of maturization" to mean "now." He told the American people that he saw "improved pluralization" in El Salvador, that terrorism could be fought with "meaningful sanctionary teeth" and that intermediate nuclear missiles were "at the vortex of cruciality." As for any worries that the public might have about such matters, his message—reduced to one-syllable words—was "leave it to Al." What he actually said was, "We must push this to a lower decibel of public fixation. I don't think there's much of a learning curve to be achieved in this area of content."

I could go on quoting examples from various fields—every profession has its growing arsenal of jargon to fire at the layman and hurl him back from its walls. But the list would be depressing and the lesson tedious. The point of raising it now is to serve notice that clutter is the enemy, whatever form it takes. It slows the reader and robs the writer of his personality, making him seem pretentious.

Beware, then, of the long word that is no better than the short word: "numerous" (many), "facilitate" (ease), "individual" (man or woman), "remainder" (rest), "initial" (first), "implement" (do), "sufficient" (enough), "attempt" (try), "referred to as" (called), and hundreds more. Beware, too, of all the slippery new fad words for which the language already has equivalents: overview and quantify, paradigm and parameter, infrastructure and interface, private sector and public sector, optimize and maximize, prioritize and potentialize. They are all weeds that will smother what you write.

Nor are all the weeds so obvious. Just as insidious are the little growths of perfectly ordinary words with which we explain how we propose to go about our explaining, or which inflate a simple preposition or conjunction into a whole windy phrase.

"I might add," "It should be pointed out," "It is interesting to note that"—how many sentences begin with these dreary clauses announcing what the writer is going to do next? If you might add, add it. If it should be pointed out, point it out. If it is interesting to note, *make* it interesting. Being told that something is interesting is the surest way of tempting the reader to find it dull; are we not all stupefied by what follows when someone says, "This will interest you"? As for the inflated prepositions and conjunctions, they are the innumerable phrases like "with the possible exception of" (except), "due to the fact that" (because), "he totally lacked the ability to" (he couldn't), "until such time as" (until), "for the purpose of" (for).

Is there any way to recognize clutter at a glance? Here's a device I used at Yale that students found helpful. I would put brackets around any component in a piece of writing that wasn't doing useful work. Often it was just one word that got bracketed: the unnecessary preposition appended to a verb ("order up"), or the adverb that carries the same meaning as the verb ("smile happily"), or the adjective that states a known fact ("tall skyscraper"). Often my brackets surrounded the little qualifiers that weaken any sentence they inhabit ("a bit," "sort of") or the announcements like "I'm tempted to say." Sometimes my brackets surrounded an entire sentence—the one that essentially repeats what the previous sentence said, or that tells the reader something he doesn't need to know or can figure out for himself. Most people's first drafts can be cut by 50 percent—they're swollen with words and phrases that do no new work whatever.

My reason for bracketing the extra words instead of crossing them out was to avoid violating the sentence. I wanted to leave it intact for the student to analyze. I was saying, "I may be wrong, but I think this can be deleted and the meaning won't be affected at all. But *you* decide: read the sentence without the bracketed material and see if it works." In the early weeks of the term I gave back papers that were infested with brackets. Entire paragraphs were bracketed. But soon the students learned to put mental brackets around their own clutter, and by the end of the term their papers were almost clean. Today many of those students are professional writers and they tell me, "I still see your brackets— they're following me through life."

You can develop the same eye. Look for the clutter in your writing and prune it ruthlessly. Be grateful for everything you can throw away. Re-examine each sentence that you put on paper. Is every word doing new work? Can any thought be expressed with more economy? Is anything pompous or pretentious or faddish? Are you hanging on to something useless just because you think it's beautiful?

Simplify, simplify.

4. Style

So much for early warnings about the bloated monsters that lie in ambush for the writer trying to put together a clean English sentence.

"But," you may say, "if I eliminate everything that you think is clutter and strip every sentence to its barest bones, will there be anything left of me?"

The question is a fair one and the fear entirely natural. Simplicity carried to its extreme might seem to point to a style where the sentences are little more sophisticated than "Dick likes Jane" and "See Spot run."

I'll answer the question first on the level of mere carpentry. Then I'll get to the larger issue of who the writer is and how to preserve his or her identity.

Few people realize how badly they write. Nobody has shown them how much excess or murkiness has crept into their style and how it obstructs what they are trying to say. If you give me an article that runs to eight pages and I tell you to cut it to four, you'll howl and say it can't be done. Then you will go home and do it, and it will be infinitely better. After that comes the hard part: cutting it to three.

The point is that you have to strip down your writing before you can build it back up. You must know what the essential tools are and what job they were designed to do. If I may labor the metaphor of carpentry, it is first necessary to be able to saw wood neatly and to drive nails. Later you can

19

bevel the edges or add elegant finials, if that is your taste. But you can never forget that you are practicing a craft that is based on certain principles. If the nails are weak, your house will collapse. If your verbs are weak and your syntax is rickety, your sentences will fall apart.

I'll admit that various nonfiction writers like Tom Wolfe and Norman Mailer have built some remarkable houses. But these are writers who spent years learning their craft, and when at last they raised their fanciful turrets and hanging gardens, to the surprise of all of us who never dreamed of such ornamentation, they knew what they were doing. Nobody becomes Tom Wolfe overnight, not even Tom Wolfe.

First, then, learn to hammer in the nails, and if what you build is sturdy and serviceable, take satisfaction in its plain strength.

But you will be impatient to find a "style"—to embellish the plain words so that readers will recognize you as someone special. You will reach for gaudy similes and tinseled adjectives, as if "style" were something you could buy at a style store and drape onto your words in bright decorator colors. (Decorator colors are the colors that decorators come in.) Resist this shopping expedition: there is no style store.

Style is organic to the person doing the writing, as much a part of him as his hair, or, if he is bald, his lack of it. Trying to add style is like adding a toupee. At first glance the formerly bald man looks young and even handsome. But at second glance—and with a toupee there is always a second glance—he doesn't look quite right. The problem is not that he doesn't look well groomed; he does, and we can only admire the wigmaker's almost perfect skill. The point is that he doesn't look like himself.

This is the problem of the writer who sets out deliberately to garnish his prose. You lose whatever it is that makes you unique. The reader will usually notice if you are putting on airs. He wants the person who is talking to him to sound genuine. Therefore a fundamental rule is: be yourself.

No rule, however, is harder to follow. It requires the writer to do two things which by his metabolism are impossible. He must relax and he must have confidence.

Telling a writer to relax is like telling a man to relax while being prodded for a possible hernia, and, as for confidence, he is a bundle of anxieties. See how stiffly he sits, glaring at the paper or the screen that awaits his words, chewing the eraser on the pencil that is so sharp because he has sharpened it so many times. A writer will do anything to avoid the act of writing. I can testify from my newspaper days that the number of trips made to the water cooler per reporter-hour far exceeds the body's known need for fluids.

What can be done to put the writer out of these miseries? Unfortunately, no cure has yet been found. I can only offer the consoling thought that you are not alone. Some days will go better than others; some will go so badly that you will despair of ever writing again. We have all had many of these days and will have many more.

Still, it would be nice to keep the bad days to a minimum, which brings me back to the matter of trying to relax.

As I said earlier, the average writer sets out to commit an act of literature. He thinks that his article must be of a certain length or it won't seem important. He thinks how august it will look in print. He thinks of all the people who will read it. He thinks that it must have the solid weight of authority. He thinks that its style must dazzle. No wonder he tightens: he is so busy thinking of his awesome responsibility to the finished article that he can't even start. Yet he vows to be worthy of the task, and, casting about for heavy phrases that would never occur to him if he weren't trying so hard to make an impression, he plunges in.

Paragraph 1 is a disaster—a tissue of ponderous generalities that seem to have come out of a machine. No *person* could have written them. Paragraph 2 is not much better. But Paragraph 3 begins to have a somewhat human quality, and by Paragraph 4 the writer begins to sound like himself. He has started to relax.

It's amazing how often an editor can simply throw away the first three or four paragraphs of an article and start with the paragraph where the writer begins to sound like himself. Not only are the first few paragraphs hopelessly impersonal and ornate; they also don't really say anything. They are a self-conscious attempt at a fancy introduction, and none is necessary.

A writer is obviously at his most natural and relaxed when he writes in the first person. Writing is, after all, a personal transaction between two people, even if it is conducted on paper, and the transaction will go well to the extent that it retains its humanity. Therefore I urge people to write in the first person—to use "I" and "me" and "we" and "us." They usually put up a fight.

"Who am I to say what *I* think?" they ask. "Or what *I* feel?"

"Who are you *not* to say what you think?" I reply. "There's only one you. Nobody else thinks or feels in exactly the same way."

"But no one cares about my opinions," they say. "It would make me feel conspicuous."

"They'll care if you tell them something interesting," I say, "and tell them in words that come naturally."

Nevertheless, getting writers to use "I" is seldom easy. They think they must somehow earn the right to reveal their emotions or their deepest thoughts. Or that it's egotistical. Or that it's undignified—a fear that hobbles the academic world. Hence the professorial use of "one" ("One finds oneself not wholly in accord with Dr. Maltby's view of the human condition") and of the impersonal "it is" ("It is to be hoped that Professor Felt's essay will find the wider audience it most assuredly deserves"). I don't want to meet "one"—he's a boring guy. I want a professor with a passion for his subject to tell me why it fascinates *him*.

I realize that there are vast regions of writing where "I" is not allowed. Newspapers don't want "I" in their news stories; many magazines don't want it in their articles; businesses and institutions don't want it in the annual reports and pamphlets that they send so profusely into the American home. Colleges don't want "I" in their term papers or dissertations, and English teachers in elementary and high schools have been taught to discourage any first-person pronoun except the literary "we" ("We see in Melville's symbolic use of the white whale . . .").

Many of these prohibitions are valid. Newspaper articles should consist of news, reported as objectively as possible. And I sympathize with teachers who don't want to give students an easy escape into opinion—"I think Hamlet was stupid"—before the students have grappled with the discipline of assessing a work on its merits and on external sources. "I" can be a self-indulgence and a cop-out.

Still, we have become a society fearful of revealing who we are. We have evolved a national language of impersonality. The institutions that seek our support by sending us their brochures tend to sound remarkably alike, though surely all of them—hospitals, schools, libraries, museums— were founded and are still sustained by men and women with different dreams and visions. Where are these people? It is hard to glimpse them among all the passive sentences that say "initiatives were undertaken" and "priorities have been identified."

Even when "I" is not permitted, it's still possible to convey a sense of I-ness. James Reston, for instance, doesn't use "I" in his columns; yet I have a good idea of what kind of person he is, and I could say the same of other essayists and reporters. Good writers are always visible just behind their words. If you aren't allowed to use "I," at least think "I" while you write, or write the first draft in the first person and then take the "I"s out. It will warm up your impersonal style.

Style, of course, is ultimately tied to the psyche, and writing has deep psychological roots. The reasons why we express ourselves as we do, or fail to express ourselves because of "writer's block," are buried partly in the subconscious mind. There are as many different kinds of writer's block as there are kinds of writers, and I have no intention of trying to untangle them here. This is a short book, and my name isn't Sigmund Freud.

But I've noticed a new reason for avoiding "I" that runs even deeper than what is not allowed or what is undignified. Americans are suddenly uncertain of what they think and unwilling to go out on a limb—an odd turn of events for a nation famous for the "rugged individualist." A generation ago our leaders told us where they stood and what they believed. Today they perform the most strenuous verbal feats to escape this fate. Watch them wriggle through television interviews without committing themselves on a single issue.

I remember President Ford trying to assure a group of visiting businessmen that his fiscal policies would work. He said: "We see nothing but increasingly brighter clouds every month." I took this to mean that the clouds were still fairly dark. Ford's sentence, however, was just misty enough to say nothing and still sedate his constituents.

But the true champ is Elliot Richardson, who held four major Cabinet positions in the 1970s—Attorney General and Secretary of Defense, Commerce and H.E.W. It's hard to know even where to begin picking from his vast trove of equivocal statements, but consider this one: "And yet, on balance, affirmative action has, I think, been a qualified success." A thirteen-word sentence with five hedging words. I give it first prize as the most wishy-washy sentence of the decade, though a close rival would be Richardson's analysis of how to ease boredom among assembly-line workers: "And so, at last, I come to the one firm conviction that I mentioned at the beginning: it is that the subject is too new for final judgments."

That's a firm conviction? Leaders who bob and weave like aging boxers don't inspire confidence—or deserve it. The same thing is true of writers. Sell yourself, and your subject will exert its own appeal. Believe in your own identity and your own opinions. Proceed with confidence, generating it, if necessary, by pure willpower. Writing is an act of ego and you might as well admit it. Use its energy to keep yourself going.

5. The Audience

Soon after you confront this matter of preserving your identity, another question will occur to you: "Who am I writing for?"

It's a fundamental question and it has a fundamental answer: you are writing for yourself. Don't try to visualize the great mass audience. There is no such audience—every reader is a different person. Don't try to guess what sort of thing editors want to publish or what you think the country is in a mood to read. Editors and readers don't know what they want to read until they read it. Besides, they're always looking for something new.

Don't worry about whether the reader will "get it" if you indulge a sudden impulse for humor or nonsense. If it amuses you in the act of writing, put it in. (It can always be taken out later, but only you can put it in.) You are writing primarily to entertain yourself, and if you go about it with confidence you will also entertain the readers who are worth writing for. If you lose the dullards back in the dust, that's where they belong.

I realize that I've raised what seems to be a paradox. Earlier I warned that the reader is an impatient bird, perched on the thin edge of distraction or sleep. Now I'm saying that you must write for yourself and not be gnawed by constant worry over whether he is tagging along behind.

I'm talking about two different problems. One is craft, the

other is attitude. The first is a question of mastering a precise skill; the second is a question of how you use that skill to express your personality.

In terms of craft, there's no excuse for losing the reader through sloppy workmanship. If he drowses off in the middle of your article because you have been careless about a technical detail, the fault is entirely yours. But on the larger issue of whether the reader likes you, or likes what you are saying, or how you are saying it, or agrees with it, or feels an affinity for your sense of humor or your vision of life, don't give him a moment's worry. You are who you are, he is who he is, and either you will get along or you won't.

Perhaps this still seems like a paradox—or at least an impossible mental act to perform. How can you think carefully about not losing the reader and still be so carefree about his opinion that you will be yourself? I can only assure you that they are two distinct processes.

First, work hard to master the tools. Simplify, prune and strive for order. Think of this as a mechanical act and soon your sentences will become cleaner. The act will never become as mechanical as, say, shaving or shampooing—you will always have to think about the various ways in which the tools can be used. But at least your sentences will be grounded in solid principles, and your chances of losing the reader will be smaller.

Think of the other process as a creative act—the expressing of who you are. Relax and say what you want to say. And since style is who you are, you only need to be true to yourself to find it gradually emerging from under the accumulated clutter and debris, growing more distinctive every day. Perhaps the style won't solidify for several years as *your* style, *your* voice—and, in fact, it shouldn't. Just as it takes time to find yourself as a person, it takes time to find yourself as a stylist, and even then, inevitably, your style will change as you grow older.

But whatever your age, be yourself when you write. Many old men still write with the zest they had in their twenties or early thirties; obviously their ideas are still young. Other old writers ramble and repeat themselves; their style is the tip-off that they have turned into redundant bores. Many college students write as if they were desiccated alumni thirty years out.

Let's look at a few writers to see the sheer pleasure with which they put onto paper their passions and their crotchets, not caring whether the reader shares them or not. The first excerpt is from "The Hen (An Appreciation)," written by E. B. White in 1944, at the height of World War II:

> Chickens do not always enjoy an honorable position among city-bred people, although the egg, I notice, goes on and on. Right now the hen is in favor. The war has deified her and she is the darling of the home front, feted at conference tables, praised in every smoking car, her girlish ways and curious habits the topic of many an excited husbandryman to whom yesterday she was a stranger without honor or allure.
>
> My own attachment to the hen dates from 1907, and I have been faithful to her in good times and bad. Ours has not always been an easy relationship to maintain. At first, as a boy in a carefully zoned suburb, I had neighbors and police to reckon with; my chickens had to be as closely guarded as an underground newspaper. Later, as a man in the country, I had my old friends in town to reckon with, most of whom regarded the hen as a comic prop straight out of vaudeville. . . . Their scorn only increased my devotion to the hen. I remained loyal, as a man would to a bride whom his family received with open ridicule. Now it is my turn to wear the smile, as I listen to the enthusiastic cackling of urbanites, who have suddenly taken up the hen socially and who fill the air

with their newfound ecstasy and knowledge and the relative charms of the New Hampshire Red and the Laced Wyandotte. You would think, from their nervous cries of wonder and praise, that the hen was hatched yesterday in the suburbs of New York, instead of in the remote past in the jungles of India.

To a man who keeps hens, all poultry lore is exciting and endlessly fascinating. Every spring I settle down with my farm journal and read, with the same glazed expression on my face, the age-old story of how to prepare a brooder house. . . .

Now there's a man writing about a subject that I have absolutely no interest in. Yet I enjoy this piece thoroughly. I like the simple beauty of its style. I like the rhythms, the unexpected but refreshing words ("deified," "allure," "cackling"), the specific details like the Laced Wyandotte and the brooder house. But mainly what I like is that this is a man telling me unabashedly about a love affair with poultry that goes back to 1907. It's written with humanity and warmth, and after three paragraphs I know quite a lot about what sort of man this hen-lover is.

Or take a writer who is almost White's opposite in terms of style, who relishes the opulent word for its very opulence and does not deify the simple sentence. Yet they are brothers in holding firm opinions and saying what they think. This is H. L. Mencken reporting on the "Monkey Trial"—the trial of John Scopes, the young teacher who taught the theory of evolution in his Tennessee classroom—in the summer of 1925:

It was hot weather when they tried the infidel Scopes at Dayton, Tenn., but I went down there very willingly, for I was eager to see something of evangelical Christianity as a going concern. In the big cities of the Republic, despite the endless efforts of consecrated men,

it is laid up with a wasting disease. The very Sunday-
school superintendents, taking jazz from the stealthy radio, shake their fire-proof legs; their pupils, moving into
adolescence, no longer respond to the proliferating hor-
mones by enlisting for missionary service in Africa, but
resort to necking instead. Even in Dayton, I found,
though the mob was up to do execution on Scopes,
there was a strong smell of antinomianism. The nine
churches of the village were all half empty on Sunday,
and weeds choked their yards. Only two or three of the
resident pastors managed to sustain themselves by their
ghostly science; the rest had to take orders for mail-
order pantaloons or work in the adjacent strawberry
fields; one, I heard, was a barber. . . . Exactly twelve
minutes after I reached the village I was taken in tow by
a Christian man and introduced to the favorite tipple of
the Cumberland Range; half corn liquor and half Coca-
Cola. It seemed a dreadful dose to me, but I found that
the Dayton illuminati got it down with gusto, rubbing
their tummies and rolling their eyes. They were all hot
for Genesis, but their faces were too florid to belong to
teetotalers, and when a pretty girl came tripping down
the main street, they reached for the places where their
neckties should have been with all the amorous enterprise of movie stars. . . .

This is pure Mencken, both in its surging momentum and
in its irreverence. At almost any page where you open one of
his books he is saying something sure to outrage the pro-
fessed pieties of his countrymen. The sanctity in which
Americans bathed their heroes, their churches and their edi-
fying laws—especially Prohibition—was a well of hypocrisy
for him that never even came close to drying up. Some of his
heaviest ammunition he hurled at Presidents and politicians—his portrait of "The Archangel Woodrow" still

scorches the pages after half a century—and as for Christian believers and clerical folk in general, they turn up unfailingly as mountebanks and boobs.

It may seem a miracle that Mencken could get away with such heresies in the 1920s, when hero worship was an American religion and the self-righteous wrath of the Bible Belt oozed from coast to coast. In fact, not only did he get away with it; he was the most revered and influential journalist of his generation. The impact that he made on subsequent writers of nonfiction is beyond measuring, and even now his topical pieces seem as fresh as if they were written yesterday.

The secret of his popularity—aside from his pyrotechnical use of the American language—was that he was obviously writing for himself and didn't worry over what the reader might think. It wasn't necessary to share his prejudices to enjoy seeing them expressed with such mirthful abandon. Mencken was never timid or evasive. He didn't kowtow to the reader or curry his favor. It takes courage to be such a writer, but it is out of such courage that revered and influential journalists are born.

Moving forward to the 1970s, here's an excerpt from *How to Survive in Your Native Land,* a book by James Herndon describing his experiences as a teacher in a California junior high school. Of all the earnest books on this subject that sprouted in America a decade ago, Herndon's is—for me— the one that best captures how it really was. His style is not quite like anybody else's, but his voice is absolutely true. Here's how the book starts:

> I might as well begin with Piston. Piston was, as a matter of description, a red-headed medium-sized chubby eighth-grader; his definitive characteristic was, however, stubbornness. Without going into a lot of detail, it became clear right away that what Piston didn't

want to do, Piston didn't do; what Piston wanted to do,
Piston did.

It really wasn't much of a problem. Piston wanted
mainly to paint, draw monsters, scratch designs on
mimeograph blanks and print them up, write an occasional horror story—some kids referred to him as The
Ghoul—and when he didn't want to do any of those, he
wanted to roam the halls and on occasion (we heard)
investigate the girls' bathrooms.

We had minor confrontations. Once I wanted everyone to sit down and listen to what I had to say—something about the way they had been acting in the halls. I
was letting them come and go freely and it was up to
them (I planned to point out) not to raise hell so that I
had to hear about it from other teachers. Sitting down
was the issue—I was determined everyone was going to
do it first, then I'd talk. Piston remained standing. I re-
ordered. He paid no attention. I pointed out that I was
talking to him. He indicated he heard me. I inquired
then why in hell didn't he sit down. He said he didn't
want to. I said I did want him to. He said that didn't
matter to him. I said do it anyway. He said why? I said
because I said so. He said he wouldn't. I said Look I
want you to sit down and listen to what I'm going to say.
He said he *was* listening. I'll listen but I won't sit down.

Well, that's the way it goes sometimes in schools. You
as teacher become obsessed with an issue—I was the
injured party, conferring, as usual, unheard-of free-
doms, and here they were as usual taking advantage. It
ain't pleasant coming in the teachers' room for coffee
and having to hear somebody say that so-and-so and so-
and-so from *your* class were out in the halls *without a
pass* and *making faces* and *giving the finger* to kids in
my class during the most *important* part of *my* lesson
about *Egypt*—and you ought to be allowed your ten-

dentious speech, and most everyone will allow it, sit down for it, but occasionally someone wises you up by refusing to submit where it isn't necessary. . . . How did any of us get into this? we ought to be asking ourselves.

Any writer who uses "ain't" and "tendentious" in the same sentence, who quotes without using quotation marks, knows what he's doing. This seemingly artless style, so full of art, is ideal for Herndon's purpose. It avoids the pretentiousness that infects so much writing by people who are doing worthy work, and it allows for a rich vein of humor, humanity and common sense. Herndon sounds like a good teacher and like a person whose company I would enjoy. But ultimately he is writing for himself: an audience of one.

"Who am I writing for?" The question that begins this chapter has irked some readers; they want me to say "Whom am I writing for?" But I can't bring myself to say it. It's just not me.

6. Words

There's a kind of writing that might be called journalese, and it's the death of freshness in anybody's style. It is the common currency of newspapers and of magazines like *People*—a mixture of cheap words, made-up words and clichés that have become so pervasive that a writer can hardly help using them automatically. You must fight these phrases off or you will sound like every hack who sits down at a typewriter. In fact, you will never make your mark as a writer unless you develop a respect for words and a curiosity about their shades of meaning that is almost obsessive. The English language is rich in strong and supple words. Take the time to root around and find the ones you want.

What is "journalese"? It's a quilt of instant words patched together out of other parts of speech. Adjectives are used as nouns ("greats," "notables"). Nouns are extended into adjectives ("insightful"). Nouns are used as verbs ("to host"), or they are chopped off to form verbs ("enthuse," "emote"), or they are padded to form verbs ("beef up," "put teeth into"). This is a world where eminent people are "famed" and their associates are "staffers," where the future is always "upcoming" and someone is forever "firing off" a note. Nobody in America has merely sent a note or a memo or a telegram in years. Famed Diplomat Henry Kissinger, who hosted foreign notables to beef up the morale of top State Department staffers, sat down and fired off a lot of notes. Notes that are fired off are always fired in anger and from a sitting position. What the weapon is I've never found out.

Here, for example, is an article from a newsmagazine that is hard to match for sheer fatigue:

> Last February, Plainclothes Patrolman Frank Serpico knocked at the door of a suspected Brooklyn heroin pusher. When the door opened a crack, Serpico shouldered his way in only to be met by a .22-cal. pistol slug crashing into his face. Somehow he survived, although there are still buzzing fragments in his head, causing dizziness and permanent deafness in his left ear. Almost as painful is the suspicion that he may well have been set up for the shooting by other policemen. For Serpico, 35, has been waging a lonely, four-year war against the routine and endemic corruption that he and others claim is rife in the New York City police department. His efforts are now sending shock waves through the ranks of New York's finest. . . . Though the impact of the commission's upcoming report has yet to be felt, Serpico has little hope that . . .

The upcoming report has yet to be felt because it is still upcoming, and as for the "permanent deafness," it's still a little early to tell. And what makes those buzzing fragments buzz? I would have thought that by now only Serpico's head would be buzzing. But apart from these lazinesses of logic, what makes the story so infinitely tired is the failure of the writer to reach for anything but the nearest cliché. "Shouldered his way," "only to be met," "crashing into his face," "waging a lonely war," "corruption that is rife," "sending shock waves," "New York's finest"—these dreary phrases constitute journalese at its worst and writing at its most banal. We know just what to expect. No surprise awaits us in the form of a bizarre word, an oblique look. We are in the hands of a hack and we know it right away.

Don't let yourself get in this position. The only way to fight it is to care deeply about words. If you find yourself writing that someone recently enjoyed a spell of illness or that a business has been enjoying a slump, stop and think how much they really enjoyed it. Notice the decisions that other writers make in their choice of words and be finicky about the ones that you select from the vast supply. The race in writing is not to the swift but to the original.

Make a habit of reading what is being written today and what has been written before. But cultivate the best writers. Don't assume that because an article is in a newspaper or a magazine it must be good. Lazy editing is endemic to American newspapers, and writers who use clichés by reflex are likely to work for editors who have seen so many clichés that they no longer even recognize them as they go limping by.

Also get in the habit of using dictionaries. My favorite for handy use is *Webster's New World Dictionary, Second College Edition,* though, like all word freaks, I own many bigger dictionaries that will reward me in their own fashion when I am on some more specialized search. (Careful writers, incidentally, cling to their copy of any Webster dictionary based on the superb Second Edition because the Third Edition is too permissive.)

If you have any doubt of what a word means, look it up. Learn its etymology and notice what curious branches its original root has put forth. See if it has any other meanings that you didn't know it had. Master the small gradations between words that seem to be synonyms. What is the difference between "cajole," "wheedle," "blandish" and "coax"? An excellent guide to these nuances is *Webster's Dictionary of Synonyms.*

And don't scorn that bulging grab bag, *Roget's Thesaurus*. It's easy to regard the book as hilarious. Look up "villain," for example, and you'll be awash in such rascality as only a lexicographer could conjure back from centuries of iniquity, obliquity, depravity, knavery, profligacy, frailty, flagrancy, infamy, immorality, corruption, wickedness, wrongdoing, backsliding and sin. You will find rogues and wretches, ruffians and riffraff, miscreants and malefactors, reprobates and rapscallions, hooligans and hoodlums, scamps and scapegraces, scoundrels and scalawags, jezebels and jades. You will find adjectives to fit them all (foul and fiendish, devilish and diabolical), and adverbs, and verbs to describe how the wrongdoers do their wrong, and cross-references leading to still other thickets of venality and vice. Still, there is no better friend to have around to nudge the memory than Roget. It saves you the time of rummaging in your own memory— that network of overloaded grooves—to find the word that's right on the tip of your tongue, where it doesn't do you any good. The *Thesaurus* is to the writer what a rhyming dictionary is to the songwriter—a reminder of all the choices— and you should use it with gratitude. If, having found the scalawag and the scapegrace, you want to know how they differ, *then* go to the dictionary.

Also bear in mind, when you are choosing words and stringing them together, how they sound. This may seem absurd: readers read with their eyes. But actually they hear what they are reading—in their inner ear—far more than you realize. Therefore such matters as rhythm and alliteration are vital to every sentence. A typical example—maybe not the best, but undeniably the nearest—is the preceding paragraph. Obviously I enjoyed making a certain arrangement of my ruffians and riffraff, my hooligans and hoodlums, and the reader enjoyed it too—far more than if I had given him a mere list. He enjoyed not only the arrangement but the effort to entertain him. He wasn't enjoying it, however, with his eyes. He was enjoying it mainly in his ear.

E. B. White makes the case cogently in *The Elements of Style* (a book that every writer should read at least once a year) when he suggests trying to rearrange any phrase that has survived for a century or two, such as Thomas Paine's "These are the times that try men's souls":

> Times like these try men's souls.
> How trying it is to live in these times!
> These are trying times for men's souls.
> Soulwise, these are trying times.

Paine's phrase is like poetry and the other four are like oatmeal, which, of course, is the divine mystery of the creative process. Yet the good writer of prose must be part poet, always listening to what he writes. E. B. White continues across the years to be my favorite stylist because I am so conscious of being with a man who cares in his bones about the cadences and sonorities of the language. I relish (in my ear) the pattern that his words make as they fall into a sentence. I try to surmise how in rewriting the sentence he reassembled it to end with a phrase that will momentarily linger, or how he chose one word over another because he was after a certain emotional weight. It is the difference between, say, "serene" and "tranquil"—one so soft, the other strangely disturbing because of the unusual "n" and "q."

Such considerations of sound and rhythm should be woven through every aspect of what you write. If all your sentences move at the same plodding gait, which even you recognize as deadly but don't know how to cure, read them aloud. (I write entirely by ear and read everything aloud before letting it go out into the world.) You will begin to hear where the trouble lies. See if you can gain variety by reversing the order of a sentence, by substituting a word that has freshness or oddity, by altering the length of your sentences so that they don't all sound as if they came out of the same computer. An occasional short sentence can carry a tremendous punch. It stays in the reader's ear.

Remember, then, that words are the only tools you will be given. Learn to use them with originality and care. Value them for their strength and their infinite diversity. And also remember: somebody out there is listening.

7. Usage

All this talk about good words and bad words brings us to a gray but important area called "usage." What is good usage? What is good English? What newly minted words is it O.K. to use, and who is to be the judge? Is it O.K. to use "O.K."?

Earlier I mentioned an incident of college students hassling the administration, and in the last chapter I described myself as a word freak. Here are two typical specimens that have crept into the language recently. "Hassle" is both a verb and a noun, meaning to give somebody a hard time, or the act of being given a hard time, and anyone who has ever been hassled by a petty bureaucrat for not properly filling out Form 35-BT will agree that it sounds exactly right. "Freak" in this new usage means an enthusiast, and there is no missing the aura of obsession that goes with calling somebody a jazz freak, or a chess freak, or a sun freak, though it would probably be pushing my luck to describe a man who compulsively visits circus sideshows as a freak freak.

Anyway, I accept both of these new arrivals wholeheartedly. I don't consider them slang, or put quotation marks around them to show that I'm mucking about in the argot of the youth culture and really know better. They're good words and we need them to express what they express. But I still won't accept "notables" and "greats" and "upcoming" and countless other newcomers. They are cheap words and we *don't* need them.

Why is one word good and another word cheap? I can't give you an answer because usage has no fixed boundaries or rules. Language is a fabric that changes from one week to another, adding new strands and dropping old ones, and even word freaks fight over what is allowable, often reaching their decision on a wholly subjective basis such as taste ("notables" is sleazy). Which still leaves the question of who our tastemakers are.

The question was confronted by the editors of a brand-new dictionary, *The American Heritage Dictionary,* at the outset of their task in the mid-1960s. They assembled a "Usage Panel" to help them appraise the new words and dubious constructions that had come knocking at the door. Which should be ushered in, which thrown out on their ear? The panel consisted of 104 men and women—mostly writers, poets, editors and teachers—who were known for caring about the language and trying to use it well. I was a member of the panel, and over the next few years I kept getting questionnaires. Would I accept "finalize" and "escalate"? How did I feel about "It's me"? Would I allow "like" to be used as a conjunction—like so many people do? How about "mighty," as in "mighty fine"?

We were told that in the dictionary our opinions would be tabulated in a separate "Usage Note" so that readers could tell how we voted. The questionnaire also left room for any comments that we might feel impelled to make—a chance that the panelists seized avidly, as we found when the dictionary was published in 1969 and our comments were released to the press. Not surprisingly, our passions ran high.

"Good God, no! Never!" cried Barbara W. Tuchman, asked about the verb "to author." Scholarship hath no fury like that of a language purist faced with sludge, and I share

Mrs. Tuchman's vow that "author" should never be authorized, just as I agree with Lewis Mumford that the adverb "good" should be "left as the exclusive property of Ernest Hemingway" and with Gerald Carson that "normalcy" should be "permitted only to admirers of the late Warren G. Harding."

But guardians of usage are only doing half their job if they merely keep the language from becoming sloppy. Any boob can rule that the suffix "wise," as in "mediawise," is boobwise, or that being "rather unique" is no more possible than being rather pregnant. The other half of the job is to help the language grow by welcoming any immigrant that will bring strength or color.

Therefore I was glad to see that 97 percent of us voted to admit "dropout," which is clean and vivid, but that only 47 percent would accept "senior citizen," which is pretentious and patronizing, typical of the pudgy new intruders from the land of sociology, where a janitor is now a maintenance engineer. I'm glad we accepted "escalate," the kind of verbal contraption which I generally dislike but which the Vietnam war gave a precise meaning, complete with overtones of blunder.

I'm glad we took into full membership all sorts of robust words that previous dictionaries had derided as "colloquial": adjectives like "rambunctious," verbs like "stall" and "trigger" and "rile," nouns like "shambles" and "tycoon" and "trek," the latter approved by 78 percent to mean any difficult trip, as in "the commuter's daily trek to Manhattan." Originally it was a Cape Dutch word applied to the Boers' arduous journey by ox wagon. But our panel evidently felt that the Manhattan commuter's daily trek is no less arduous.

Still, 22 percent of us were unwilling to let "trek" slip into general usage. This was the virtue of revealing how our panel voted—it put our agreements and our discords on display, and now any writer who is in doubt can conduct himself accordingly. Thus our 95 percent vote against "myself," as in "He invited Mary and myself to dinner," a word condemned as "prissy," "horrible" and "a genteelism," ought to warn off anyone who doesn't want to be prissy, horrible and genteel. As Red Smith put it, "'Myself' is the refuge of idiots taught early that 'me' is a dirty word."

On the other hand, only 66 percent of our panel rejected the verb "to contact," and only half opposed the split infinitive and the verbs "to fault" and "to bus." So only 50 percent of your readers will fault you if you decide to voluntarily call your school board and to bus your children to another town. If you contact your school board you risk your reputation by another 16 percent. Our apparent rule of thumb was stated by Theodore M. Bernstein: "We should apply the test of convenience. Does the word fill a real need? If it does, let's give it a franchise." I agree with Bernstein. "Hassle," for instance, fills a real need.

All of this merely confirms what lexicographers have always known: that the laws of usage are relative, bending with the taste of the lawmaker. One of our panelists, Katherine Anne Porter, called "O.K." a "detestable vulgarity" and claimed that she had never spoken the word in her life, whereas I freely admit that I have spoken the word "O.K." "Most," as in "most everyone," was scorned as "cute farmer talk" by Isaac Asimov and embraced as a "good English idiom" by Virgil Thomson.

"Regime," meaning any administration, as in "the Truman regime," drew the approval of most everyone on the panel, as did "dynasty." But they drew the wrath of Jacques Barzun, who said, "These are technical terms, you blasted non-historians!" Probably I gave my O.K. to "regime" when I filled out the questionnaire. Now, chided by Barzun for imprecision, I think it looks like journalese. One of the words that *I* railed against was "personality," as in a "TV personality." But now I wonder if it isn't the only word for that vast swarm of people who are famous for being famous—and, possibly, for nothing else. What, for instance, do the Gabor sisters really *do?*

In the end it comes down to one question: What is "correct" usage? We have no king to establish the King's English; we only have the President's English—which we don't want. Webster, long a defender of the faith, muddied the waters in 1961 with its permissive Third Edition, which argued that almost anything goes as long as somebody uses it, noting that "ain't" is "used orally in most parts of the U.S. by many cultivated speakers."

Just where Webster cultivated those speakers I ain't sure. Nevertheless it's true that the spoken language is looser than the written language, and *The American Heritage Dictionary* properly put its question to us in both forms. Often we allowed an oral idiom which we forbade in print as too informal, fully realizing, however, that "the pen must at length comply with the tongue," as Samuel Johnson said, and that today's spoken garbage may be tomorrow's written gold. Certainly the growing acceptance of the split infinitive, or of the preposition at the end of a sentence, proves that formal syntax can't—or shouldn't—hold the fort forever against a speaker's more comfortable way of getting the same thing said. A sentence is a fine thing to put a preposition at the end of. As for "It's me," who would defend to the death "It is I"? Only a purity freak.

Our panel recognized that correctness can even vary within a particular word. We voted heavily against "cohort," for instance, as a synonym for "colleague," except where the tone was jocular. Thus a professor would not be among his cohorts at a faculty meeting, but they would abound at his college reunion, wearing funny hats. We rejected "too" as a synonym for "very," as in "His health is not too good." Whose health is? But we approved it in wry or humorous use, as in "He was not too happy when she ignored him."

These may seem like picayune distinctions. They're not. They are signals to the reader that you are sensitive to the many shadings of usage. "Too," when substituted for "very," is clutter—"He didn't feel too much like going shopping"— and should be cut out. But the wry example in the previous paragraph is worthy of Ring Lardner. It adds a tinge of sarcasm that wouldn't otherwise be there.

Did any pattern emerge from the opinions of our panel when we finally ended our task, or were we just flexing our prejudices and pedantries? Luckily, a pattern did emerge, and it offers a guideline that is still useful. In general we turned out to be liberal in accepting new words and phrases, but conservative in grammar.

It would be foolish, for instance, to reject a word as perfect as "dropout," or to pretend that countless words and phrases are not entering the gates of correct usage every day, borne on the winds of science and technology, fad and fashion, social change and social concern: "meltdown," "skyjacker," "wetlands," "software," "macho," "yuppie," "fast track," "flip side," "state-of-the-art," "pro-life," "pro-choice" and hundreds of others. Nor should we forget all the wonderfully short words invented by the counterculture in the 1960s as a way of lashing back at the bloated verbiage of the Establishment: "bag," "scene," "trip," "rap," "crash," "trash," "fuzz," "funky," "split," "rip-off," "vibes," "downer," "bummer," et al. If brevity is a prize, these were sure winners. The only trouble with accepting words that entered the language overnight is that they have a tendency to leave as abruptly as they came. The "happenings" of the late 1960s no longer happen, "out of sight" is out of sight, nobody does his "thing" anymore, and "relevant" has been hooted out of the room. Be vigilant, therefore, about instant change. The writer who cares about usage must always know the quick from the dead.

As for the area where our Usage Panel was conservative,

we strictly upheld most of the classic distinctions in grammar—"can" and "may," "fewer" and "less," "eldest" and "oldest," etc.—and decried the classic errors, insisting that "flout" still doesn't mean "flaunt," no matter how many writers flaunt their ignorance by flouting the rule, and that "fortuitous" still means "accidental," "disinterested" still means "impartial," and "infer" doesn't mean "imply."

Here we were motivated by our love of the language's beautiful precision. We hate to see our favorite tools mistreated. As Dwight Macdonald put it, "Simple illiteracy is no basis for linguistic evolution." This is where correct usage will win or lose you the readers you would most like to win. Know the difference between a "reference" and an "allusion," between "connive" and "conspire," between "compare with" and "compare to." If you must use "comprise," use it right.

"I choose always the grammatical form unless it sounds affected," explained Marianne Moore, and that finally is where our Usage Panel took its stand. We were not pedants, so hung up on correctness that we didn't want the language to keep refreshing itself with phrases like "hung up." But that didn't mean we had to accept every atrocity that has come stumbling in, like "hopefully."

Meanwhile the battle continues. Several years ago the Usage Panel was reconstituted, with new members added, and we continue to receive ballots soliciting our opinion on new words and locutions: verbs like "definitize" ("Congress definitized a proposal") and "attrit" ("to attrit the population base of the enemy"), nouns like "affordables" and "collectibles," colloquialisms like "the bottom line" and "up front," and strays like "into" ("He's into backgammon and she's into jogging").

Fortunately, it no longer takes a panel of experts to notice that jargon is inundating many areas of American life, especially government, business, education and the social sciences. President Carter signed an executive order directing that federal regulations be written "simply and clearly"; corporations and law firms have hired consultants to make their prose less murky and specialized, and even the insurance industry is trying to rewrite its policies to tell us in less disastrous English what redress will be ours when disaster strikes. Whether these efforts will do much good I wouldn't want to bet, nor, probably, would Jimmy the Greek. Still, there is comfort in the sight of so many people standing Canute-like on the beach, trying to hold back the tide. That's where all careful writers ought to be, looking at every new piece of debris that washes up and asking "Do we need it?"

I remember the first time somebody asked me—only a few years ago—"How does that impact you?" I had always thought that "impact" was a noun, except in dentistry, which I try not to think of at all. Then I began to meet "de-impact," usually in connection with programs to de-impact the effects of a hard winter or some other adversity. Nouns now turn overnight into verbs. We target goals and we access facts. My train conductor announces that the train won't platform in Stamford.

I see that Detroit is downsizing its cars but still hoping to attract upscale customers. (Small Cadillacs for rich people.) It's part of an ongoing effort to save energy. All efforts in America today are "ongoing." So are all programs and investigations. So, in fact, are all people and all forms of life; when we cease to be ongoing we're dead. "Ongoing" is a jargon word that is wholly unnecessary except to raise morale. We face our daily job with more zest if the boss reminds us that it's an ongoing project; we give more willingly to institutions if they have targeted our funds for ongoing improvements.

One hospital wrote me about its plan to "modernize, expand and reconfigure" its facilities. When did "reconfigure" poke its haughty nose into our ongoing life? We were all doing fine without it. I would certainly hope that any architect trying to modernize a facility would move things around in response to new needs. "Reconfigure" gives his work the necessary grandeur to raise the necessary cash. Otherwise a donor might fall prey to "disincentivization."

I could go on. I have enough horrible examples to fill a book, but it's not a book I would want anyone to read. We're still left with the question: What is good usage? Perhaps one helpful way of looking at the question is to try to separate usage from jargon.

I would say, for instance, that "prioritize" is jargon—a pompous new verb that sounds more important than "rank"—and that "bottom line" is usage, a metaphor borrowed from the world of bookkeeping that conveys an image we can picture. As every businessman knows, the bottom line is the one that ultimately matters. It tells how things stand after all the gains and losses have been added up. If someone says, "The bottom line is that we just can't work together," we know what he means. I don't much like the phrase, but the bottom line is that it's probably here to stay.

New usages also arrive with new political events. Just as Vietnam gave us "escalate," Watergate gave us a whole lexicon of words connoting obstruction and deceit, such as "stonewall," "deep-six" and "launder." It's a fitting irony that under Richard Nixon "launder" became a dirty word. Today when we hear that someone laundered his funds in Mexico to hide the origin of the money and the route it took, the word has a precise meaning. It's short, it's vivid, and we need it. I accept "launder" and "stonewall"; I don't accept "prioritize" and "disincentive."

I would suggest a similar guideline for separating good English from technical English. It's the difference between, say, "printout" and "input." A printout is a specific object that a computer emits. Before the advent of computers it wasn't needed. Now it is. But it has stayed where it belongs—in the world where computers are used. Not so with "input," which was invented to describe the information that's fed to a computer. The word has broken out of the machine and run wild. Our input is sought on every subject, from diets and pets to philosophical discourse ("I'd like your input on whether God really exists").

I don't want to give somebody my input and get his feedback, though I'd be glad to offer my ideas. To me, good usage consists of using good words if they already exist—as they usually do—to express myself clearly and simply to someone else. You might say it's how I try to verbalize the interpersonal.

PART **II**

Forms

8. Nonfiction as the New American Literature

One weekend not long ago I went to Buffalo to talk at a writers' conference that had been organized by a group of women writers in that city. They were serious about their craft, and the books and articles they had written were solid and useful. They asked me if I would take part in a radio talk show earlier in the week to publicize the conference—they would be with the host in the studio and I would be on a telephone hookup from my apartment in New York.

The appointed evening arrived, and my phone rang, and the host came on and greeted me with the strenuous joviality of his trade. He said he had three lovely ladies in the studio with him and he was eager to find out what we all thought of the present state of literature and what advice we had for all his listeners who were members of the literati and who had literary ambitions themselves. This hearty introduction dropped like a stone in our midst, and none of the three lovely ladies said anything, which I thought was the proper response. The silence lengthened, and finally I said, "I think we should start by banishing all further mention of the words 'literature' and 'literary' and 'literati.'" I knew that the host had been briefed about what kind of writers we were and what we wanted to discuss. But he had no other frame of reference. "Tell me," he said, "what insights do you all have about the literary experience in America today?" Silence also

greeted this question. Finally I said, "We're here to talk
about the craft of writing."

He didn't know what to make of that, and he began to
invoke the names of authors like Ernest Hemingway and
Saul Bellow and William Styron, whom we surely regarded
as literary giants. We said that those writers didn't happen to
be our models, and we mentioned people like Lewis Thomas
and Joan Didion and Stephen Jay Gould and Gary Wills and
George Orwell and John McPhee. He had never heard of
any of them. One of the women mentioned Tom Wolfe's *The
Right Stuff*, and he hadn't heard of that. I mentioned Russell
Baker's *Growing Up*, which had just been published to great
acclaim. I said that it was not only a superb memoir, but a
classic book about the Depression. He hadn't heard of that,
either. We explained that these were writers we admired for
their ability to harness the issues and concerns of the day.

"But don't you want to write anything literary?" our host
said. The three women said they felt that they were already
doing satisfying work. That brought the program to another
halt, and the host began to accept phone calls from his listeners, all of whom were interested in the craft of writing
and wanted to know how we went about it. "And yet, in the
stillness of the night," the host said to several callers, "don't
you ever dream of writing the great American novel?" They
didn't. They had no such dreams—in the stillness of the
night or at any other time. It was one of the all-time lousy
radio talk shows.

The story sums up a situation that any practitioner of nonfiction will recognize. Those of us who are trying to write
well about the world we live in, or to teach students to write
well about the world *they* live in, are caught in a time warp,
where literature by definition consists of forms that were
certified as "literary" in the nineteenth century: novels and
short stories and poems. But in fact these have become quite
rarefied forms in American life. The great preponderance of

what writers now write and sell, what book and magazine publishers publish, and what readers demand is nonfiction.

The shift can be documented by all kinds of examples. One, for instance, is the history of the Book-of-the-Month Club. When the club was founded in 1926 by Harry Scherman, Americans had little access to new literature and were mainly reading junk like *Ben-Hur*. Scherman's idea was that any town that had a post office had the equivalent of a bookstore, and he began sending the best new books to his newly recruited readers all over the country. Much of what he sent was fiction. The list of main selections chosen by the club from 1926 through 1941 is heavily laced with novelists: Ellen Glasgow, Sinclair Lewis, Virginia Woolf, John Galsworthy, Elinor Wylie, Ignazio Silone, Rosamond Lehmann, Edith Wharton, Somerset Maugham, Willa Cather, Booth Tarkington, Isak Dinesen, James Gould Cozzens, Thornton Wilder, Sigrid Undset, Ernest Hemingway, William Saroyan, John P. Marquand, John Steinbeck and many others. That was the high tide of "literature" in America. In fact, members of the Book-of-the-Month Club hardly heard the approach of World War II. Their first whiff of it came in 1940 with *Mrs. Miniver*, a stiff-upper-lip novel about the early days of the Battle of Britain.

All of this changed with Pearl Harbor. World War II sent seven million Americans overseas and opened their eyes to reality: to new places and issues and events. After they came home the trend was reinforced by the advent of television. People who saw reality every evening in their living room suddenly lost patience with the slower rhythms and glancing allusions of the novelist. Overnight, America became a fact-minded nation. Since 1946 the Book-of-the-Month Club's million-odd members have predominantly demanded—and therefore, needless to say, received—works of nonfiction.

Magazines were swept along on the same current. The *Saturday Evening Post*, which had long spoon-fed its readers a heavy diet of short stories by writers who all seemed to have three names, like Clarence Budington Kelland and Octavus Roy Cohen, reversed the ratio in the early 1960s. Ninety percent of the magazine was allotted to nonfiction articles, with just one short story by a three-named author thrown into the mixture to keep the faithful from feeling abandoned. It was the beginning of a golden era of nonfiction—especially in *Life*, which ran finely crafted articles every week; in *The New Yorker*, which elevated the form by originating such landmarks of modern American writing as Rachel Carson's *Silent Spring* and Truman Capote's *In Cold Blood*; and in *Harper's*, which commissioned such remarkable pieces as Norman Mailer's *Armies of the Night*. Nonfiction, in short, became the new American literature.

Today there is no area of life that isn't being made accessible to the public by writers writing with high seriousness and grace. I think, for instance, of Lewis Thomas and Berton Roueché in medicine and biology, of Stephen Jay Gould in natural science and evolution, of John McPhee in geology and the environment, of Tom Wolfe in aeronautics and space, of Freeman Dyson in nuclear weaponry and disarmament—writers who manage to explain science and technology with both precision and humanity. And I think of stars in many other fields: Roger Angell (baseball), Joan Didion (popular culture), Gloria Steinem (women's issues), Jane Jacobs (urban issues), Robert Coles (sociology), John Kenneth Galbraith (economics), Bruce Chatwin (travel), Gary Wills (politics), Frances FitzGerald (education), Janet Malcolm (psychoanalysis), Michael Herr (Vietnam), Michael Arlen (television), Wendell Berry (nature)—that's just the beginning of a long list.

Add to it all the fields that were once regarded as academic, like anthropology, which have become the domain of the informed nonfiction writer and the broadly curious reader. Add all the excellent writing now being done in history and biography. Historians like Barbara Tuchman and William L. Shirer, biographers like Robert Caro and David McCullough, and historical scholars like Daniel Boorstin exert their strong hold over us because they not only bring back the past but make us think about the present. My roster of the new literature, in short, would include all the writers who come bearing knowledge and presenting it clearly and making an arrangement of it that constitutes a thoughtful act of writing. In an age when survival is tenuous and events so often outrun our ability to make sense of them, these are important writers.

I'm not saying that fiction is dead or that I'm against it. Obviously the novelist can take us into hidden places where no other writer can go: into the deep emotions, into the texture of daily existence, into the interior life. What I am saying is that I have no patience with the snobbery that accompanies "literature"—the snobbery which says that nonfiction is only journalism by another name, and that journalism by any name is a dirty word. While we're redefining literature, let's also redefine journalism. Journalism is writing that first appears in any periodic journal. Lewis Thomas' first two books—*Lives of a Cell* and *The Medusa and the Snail*—were first written as essays for the *New England Journal of Medicine*. In fact, almost all the writers I just mentioned wrote their books first as journalism. Historically, good journalism becomes good literature in this country. H. L. Mencken, Ring Lardner, Joseph Mitchell, Edmund Wilson and dozens of other major American writers were working journalists long before they were canonized in the church of literature. They simply did what they did best and never worried about how it was defined.

Ultimately every writer must follow the path that feels most comfortable. For most people who are learning to write, that path is nonfiction. It enables them to write about what they know or can observe or can find out. This is especially true of young people—they will write far more willingly about experiences that touch their own lives because that's what interests them. Motivation is at the heart of writing. If nonfiction is where you do your best writing, or your best teaching of writing, don't be buffaloed into the notion that it's an inferior species. The only important distinction is between good writing and bad writing. Good writing is good writing, whatever form it takes and whatever we call it.

9. Unity

You learn to write by writing. It's a truism, but what makes it a truism is that it's true, and it can't be repeated often enough. The only way to learn to write is to force yourself to produce a certain number of words on a regular basis.

If you went to work for a newspaper that required you to write two or three articles every day, you would be a better writer after six months. You wouldn't necessarily be writing well—your style might still be pedestrian, full of clutter and clichés. But at least you would be exercising your powers of putting the English language on paper, gaining confidence, and identifying the commonest problems.

All writing is ultimately a question of solving a problem. It may be a problem of where to obtain the facts, or how to organize the material. It may be a problem of approach or attitude, tone or style. Whatever it is, it has to be confronted and solved.

Sometimes you will despair of finding the right solution—or any solution. You will think: "If I live to be ninety I'll never get out of this mess I'm in." I've often thought it myself. But when I finally do solve the problem it's because I have written millions and millions of words. Like a surgeon doing his five hundredth appendix operation, I've been there before and have a surer instinct than the beginner about how to fix what has gone wrong.

So now I'll put you to actual writing. First I wanted to

give you a set of principles and to suggest the enormous range of opportunities that nonfiction offers to anyone writing in America today. Now the task is to apply these principles to the various forms that nonfiction can take: the interview, the travel piece, technical writing, business writing, sports, criticism, humor and all the hybrid species that can result from mixing them together. Every form has its special pitfalls. But all of them share one horrible problem: how to get started. No element of writing causes so much anguish as "the lead," and with almost no further ado I will try to wrestle it into partial submission. The only ado that I will first commit is to suggest that before you struggle with the lead you make certain decisions about what tone you want to adopt. Get your unities straight.

Unity is the anchor of good writing. It not only keeps the reader from straggling off in all directions; it satisfies his subconscious need for order and assures him that all is well at the helm. Therefore choose from among the many variables and stick to your choice.

One choice is unity of pronoun. Are you going to write in the first person as a participant or in the third person as an observer? Or even in the second person, that darling of sportswriters hung up on Hemingway ("You knew this had to be the most spine-tingling clash of giants you'd ever seen from a pressbox seat, and you weren't just some green kid who was still wet behind the ears")?

Unity of tense is another choice. Most people write mainly in the past tense ("I went up to Boston the other day"), but some people write agreeably in the present ("I'm sitting in the dining car of the Yankee Limited and we're pulling into Boston"). What is not agreeable is to switch back and forth. I'm not saying that you can't use more than one tense. Obviously the whole purpose of tenses is to enable a writer to deal with time in its various gradations from the past to the hypothetical future ("When I telephoned my girl from the

Boston station I realized that if I had written to tell her I would be coming she would have waited for me"). What I am saying is that you must choose the tense in which you are *principally* going to address the reader, no matter how many glances you may take backward or forward along the way.

Another choice is unity of mood. You might want to talk to the reader in the casual and chatty voice that *The New Yorker* has so strenuously refined. Or you might want to approach him with a certain formality to describe a serious event or to acquaint him with a set of important facts. Both tones are acceptable. In fact, *any* tone is acceptable. But don't mix two or three.

Such fatal mixtures are common in the nonfiction of writers who haven't yet learned control. Travel writing is a conspicuous case. "My wife, Ann, and I had always wanted to visit Hong Kong," the writer begins, his blood astir with reminiscence, "and one day last spring we found ourselves looking at an airline poster and I said, 'Let's go!' The kids were grown up or in school," he continues, and proceeds to describe in genial detail how they stopped off in Hawaii and had such a comical time changing their money at the Hong Kong airport and finding their hotel. Fine. He is a real person taking us along on a real trip, and we can identify with him and Ann.

Suddenly he turns into a travel brochure. "Hong Kong affords many fascinating experiences to the curious sightseer," he writes. "One can ride the picturesque ferry from Kowloon and gawk at the myriad sampans as they scuttle across the teeming harbor, or take a day's trip to browse in the alleys of fabled Macao with its colorful history as a den of smuggling and intrigue. You will want to take the quaint funicular that climbs . . ." Then we get back to him and Ann and their efforts to eat at Chinese restaurants, and again all is well. Everyone is interested in food and we are being told about a personal quest.

Then suddenly the writer is a guidebook: "To enter Hong Kong it is necessary to have a valid passport but no visa is required. You should definitely be immunized against smallpox and you would also be well advised to consult your physician with regard to a possible inoculation for typhoid. The climate in Hong Kong is seasonable except in July and August when . . ." Our writer is gone, and so is Ann, and so— very soon—are we.

It's not that the scuttling sampans and the smallpox shots should not be included. What annoys us is that the writer never decided what kind of article he wanted to write or how he wanted to approach us. He comes at us in many guises, depending on what kind of material he is trying to purvey. Instead of controlling his material, he is allowing his material to control him. This wouldn't happen if he took time to establish certain unities.

Therefore ask yourself some basic questions before you start. For example: "In what capacity am I going to address the reader?" (Reporter? Provider of information? Average man or woman?) "What pronoun and tense am I going to use?" "What style?" (Impersonal reportorial? Personal but formal? Personal and casual?) "What attitude am I going to take toward the material?" (Involved? Detached? Judgmental? Ironic? Amused?) "How much do I want to cover?" "What one point do I really want to make?"

The last two questions are more important than they might seem. Most nonfiction writers have a definitiveness complex. They feel that their article must be the last word and the most comprehensive word. It's a commendable impulse, but there is no definitive article. What you think is definitive today will turn undefinitive by tomorrow, and the writer who doggedly pursues every last fact will find himself pursuing the rainbow and never settling down to write. Decide what corner of your subject you are going to bite off, and be content to cover it well and stop. You can always come back another day and bite off another corner.

As for what point you want to make, I'll state as a rule of thumb that every successful piece of nonfiction should leave the reader with one provocative thought that he didn't have before. Not two thoughts, or five—just one. So try to decide what point you most want to leave in the reader's mind. It will not only give you a better idea of what route you ought to follow and what destination you hope to reach; it will also affect your decision about tone and attitude. Some points are best made by dry understatement, some by heavy irony.

Once you have these unities decided, there is no material that you can't work into your frame. If the man writing about Hong Kong had chosen to write solely in the conversational vein about what he and Ann thought and did, he would have found a natural way to weave into his narrative whatever he wanted to tell us about the Kowloon ferry and the local weather. His personality and purpose would be intact, and his article would hold together.

Now it's possible that you will make these prior decisions and then discover that they were not the right ones. The material seems to be leading you in an unexpected direction where you are more comfortable writing in a different tone. This is not abnormal—the very act of writing will often summon out of the brain some cluster of thoughts or memories that you didn't anticipate. Don't fight such a current if it feels right. Trust your material if it is taking you into terrain that you didn't intend to enter but where the vibrations are good. Adjust your style and your mood accordingly and proceed to whatever destination you reach. Don't ever become the prisoner of a preconceived plan. Writing is no respecter of blueprints—it's too subjective a process, too full of surprises.

Of course if this happens, the second part of your article

will be badly out of joint with the first. But at least you'll
know which part is truest to your instincts. Then it's just a
matter of making repairs. Go back to the beginning and rewrite it so that the mood and style are consistent.

There's nothing in such a method to be ashamed of. Scissors and paste are honorable writers' tools. Just remember
that all the unities must be fitted into the edifice that you
finally put together, however backwardly they may fall into
place, or it will soon come tumbling down.

10. The Lead

The most important sentence in any article is the first one. If it doesn't induce the reader to proceed to the second sentence, your article is dead. And if the second sentence doesn't induce him to continue to the third sentence, it's equally dead. Of such a progression of sentences, each tugging the reader forward until he is safely hooked, a writer constructs that fateful unit: the "lead."

How long should the lead be? One or two paragraphs? Four or five? There is no pat answer. Some leads hook the reader with just a few well-baited sentences; others amble on for several pages, exerting a slow but steady pull. Every article poses a different problem, and the only valid test is: Does it work? Your lead may not be the best of all possible leads, but if it does the job that it's supposed to do, be thankful and proceed.

Sometimes the length may depend on the audience that you are writing for. Readers of *The New Yorker* or of a literary review, for instance, expect the writer to start somewhat discursively, and they will stick with him for the pleasure of wondering where he will emerge as he moves in leisurely circles toward his eventual point. But I urge you not to count on the reader to stick around. He is a fidgety fellow who wants to know—very soon—what's in it for him.

Therefore the lead must capture the reader immediately and force him to keep reading. It must cajole him with freshness or novelty or paradox, or with humor, or with surprise, or with an unusual idea, or an interesting fact, or a question. Anything will do as long as it nudges his curiosity and tugs at his sleeve.

Next the lead must do some real work. It must provide a few hard details that tell the reader why the piece was written and why he ought to read it. But don't dwell on the reason. Coax the reader a little more; keep him inquisitive.

Continue to build. Every paragraph should amplify the one that preceded it. Give more thought to adding solid detail and less to entertaining the reader. But take special care with the last sentence of each paragraph—it's the crucial springboard to the next paragraph. Try to give that sentence an extra twist of humor or surprise, like the periodic "snapper" in the routine of a stand-up comic. Make the reader smile and you've got him for at least one paragraph more.

Let's look at a few leads that vary in pace but are alike in maintaining pressure. I'll start with three columns of my own that first appeared in, respectively, *Life, The Saturday Evening Post* and *Look*—three magazines which, judging by the comments of readers, found their consumers mainly in barbershops, hairdressing salons and airplanes ("I was getting a haircut the other day and I saw your article"). I mention this as a reminder that far more periodical reading is done in America under the dryer than under the reading lamp, so there isn't much time for the writer to fool around.

I don't claim that these are the three best leads I could have found; I only know that they work. The first is the lead of a piece called "Block That Chickenfurter":

I've often wondered what goes into a hot dog. Now I know and I wish I didn't.

Two very short sentences. But it would be hard not to continue to the second paragraph:

My trouble began when the Department of Agriculture published the hot dog's ingredients—everything that may legally qualify—because it was asked by the poultry industry to relax the conditions under which the ingredients might also include chicken. In other words, can a chickenfurter find happiness in the land of the frank?

One sentence that explains the incident that the column is based on. Then a snapper to restore the easygoing tone.

Judging by the 1,066 mainly hostile answers that the Department got when it sent out a questionnaire on this point, the very thought is unthinkable. The public mood was most felicitously caught by the woman who replied: "I don't eat feather meat of no kind."

Another fact and another smile. Whenever you're lucky enough to get a quotation as funny as that one, find a way to use it—preferably at the end of a paragraph.

The article then specifies what the Department of Agriculture says may go into a hot dog—a list that includes "the edible part of the muscle of cattle, sheep, swine or goats, in the diaphragm, in the heart or in the esophagus . . . [but not including] the muscle found in the lips, snout or ears."

From there it progresses—not without an involuntary reflex around the esophagus—into an account of the controversy between the poultry interests and the frankfurter interests, which in turn leads to the point that Americans will eat anything that even remotely resembles a hot dog. Implicit at the end is the larger point that Americans don't know, or care, what goes into the food they eat. The style of the article has remained casual and touched with humor throughout. But its content turns out to be more serious than the reader expected when he was drawn into it by a somewhat whimsical lead.

Here's another lead, from an article that was called "Does He or Doesn't He?":

> Until this year I have always wanted to smell as good as the next man. But now the next man wants to smell too good. The boom in male cosmetics is sweeping America at such speed—sales went over half a billion dollars in 1965 alone and are growing fast—that one of the country's most popular entertainers recently refused to tell the name of the scent that he was wearing. Too many other men, he explained, would also start to wear it.
>
> That entertainer's secret would be safe with me. He could tell me the name of his scent tomorrow and I swear I wouldn't call up my pharmacy. Nor do I own a single face cream, and I've never been to any of the men's "hair stylists" for a tinting or a spray. I go to a funny old-fashioned barber who just cuts my hair and doesn't try to make me look younger than when I went in. If anything, his conversation sends me out older.

The last sentence does no real work—it's a tiny joke and not a very good one. But it propels the reader on to the third paragraph, where the article gets down to business:

> All of this makes me a member of America's newest minority group: an adult male untouched by rejuvenating lotions, fragrances and dyes. "A case of galloping vanity has hit men in this country," Eugenia Sheppard writes, "and any minute now there'll be masks, moisturizers, home hair coloring and hair sprays for men."
>
> That minute is almost here. Hardly a day goes by when I don't read in the paper or see in a TV commercial some new evidence that . . .

The article goes on to document the growing American belief that a man who looks young and glossy is more competent than his visibly aging colleague. From there it veers off, in a turn just sharp enough to catch the reader off balance, to arrive at the sober point it intended all along to reach—that this is a crazy way for a society to operate. In style the unities continue to be intact: "I don't want to touch—or retouch—a hair of the gray heads that ponder my financial, legal and medical affairs. . . . I like to think that every one of their gray hairs was honorably earned, every facial line etched by a mistake that they will not make again." But the substance is far deeper than the reader anticipated when he was being pampered through the first few paragraphs. What remains with him is not the lead, but the point.

A slightly slower lead, luring the reader more with curiosity than with humor, introduced a piece called "Thank God for Nuts":

> By any reasonable standard, nobody would want to look twice—or even once—at the piece of slippery elm bark from Clear Lake, Wisc., birthplace of pitcher Burleigh Grimes, that is on display at the National Baseball Museum and Hall of Fame in Cooperstown, N.Y. As the label explains, it is the kind of bark that Grimes chewed during games "to increase saliva for throwing the spitball. When wet, the ball sailed to the plate in deceptive fashion." This would seem to be one of the least interesting facts available in America today.
>
> But baseball fans can't be judged by any reasonable standard. We are obsessed by the minutiae of the game and nagged for the rest of our lives by the memory of players we once saw play. No item is therefore too trivial that puts us back in touch with them. I am just old enough to remember Burleigh Grimes and his well-moistened pitches sailing deceptively to the plate, and when I found his bark I studied it as intently as if I had come upon the Rosetta Stone. "So *that's* how he did it,"

I thought, peering at the odd botanical relic. "Slippery elm! I'll be damned."

This was only one of several hundred encounters that I had with my own boyhood as I prowled through the Museum, a handsome brick building on Main Street, only a peanut bag's throw from the pasture where Abner Doubleday allegedly invented the game in 1839. Probably no other museum is so personal a pilgrimage to our past . . .

The reader is now safely hooked, and the hardest part of the writer's job is over.

One reason for citing this lead is to point out that salvation often lies not in the writer's style but in some odd fact he was able to discover. I remember that I went up to Cooperstown and spent a whole afternoon in the museum, taking voluminous notes. Jostled everywhere by nostalgia, I gazed with reverence at Lou Gehrig's locker and Bobby Thomson's game-winning bat. I sat in a grandstand seat brought from the Polo Grounds, dug my unspiked soles into the home plate from Ebbets Field, and dutifully copied all the labels and captions that might be useful.

"These are the shoes that touched home plate as Ted finished his journey around the bases," said the label identifying the shoes worn by Ted Williams when he hit a home run on his last time at bat. The shoes were in much better shape than the pair—rotted open at the sides—that belonged to Walter Johnson. But again the caption provided exactly the kind of justifying fact that a baseball nut would want. "My feet must be comfortable when I'm out there a-pitching," the great Walter said.

The museum closed at five and I returned to my motel secure in my memories and my research. But instinct told me to go back the next morning for a final tour, and it was only then that I noticed Burleigh Grimes' slippery elm bark, which struck me as an ideal lead. It still does.

One moral of this story is that you should always collect more material than you will eventually use. Every article is strong in proportion to the surplus of details from which you can choose the few that will serve you best—if you don't go on gathering facts forever. At some point you must decide to stop researching and start writing.

An even more important moral is to look for your material everywhere, not just by reading the obvious sources and interviewing the obvious people. Look at signs and at billboards and at all the junk written along the American roadside. Read the labels on our packages and the instructions on our toys, the claims on our medicines and the graffiti on our walls.

Read the fillers, so rich in self-esteem, that come spilling out of your monthly statement from the electric company and the telephone company and the bank. Read menus and catalogues and second-class mail. Nose about in obscure crannies of the newspaper, like the Sunday real estate section—you can tell the temper of a society by what patio accessories it wants. Our daily landscape is thick with absurd messages and portents. Notice them. They not only have a certain social significance; they are often just quirky enough to make a lead that's different from everybody else's.

And speaking of everybody else's lead, there are several categories that I'd be glad never to see again. One is the future archaeologist: "When some future archaeologist stumbles upon the remains of our civilization a thousand years from now, what will he make of the jukebox?" I'm tired of him already and he's not even here. I'm also tired of the visitor from Mars: "If a creature from Mars landed on our planet tomorrow, he would be amazed to see hordes of scantily clad earthlings lying on the sand and barbecuing their skins." And I'm tired of the cute event that just happened to happen "one day not long ago" or on a conveniently recent Saturday afternoon. "One day not long ago a small button-nosed boy was walking with his dog, Terry, in a field outside Paramus, N.J., when he saw something that looked strangely like a balloon rising out of the ground." Let's retire the future archaeologist and the man from Mars and the button-nosed boy. Try to give your lead a freshness of perception or detail.

Consider this lead, by Joan Didion, on a piece called "7000 Romaine, Los Angeles 38":

> Seven Thousand Romaine Street is in that part of Los Angeles familiar to admirers of Raymond Chandler and Dashiell Hammett: the underside of Hollywood, south of Sunset Boulevard, a middle-class slum of "model studios" and warehouses and two-family bungalows. Because Paramount and Columbia and Desilu and the Samuel Goldwyn studios are nearby, many of the people who live around here have some tenuous connection with the motion-picture industry. They once processed fan photographs, say, or knew Jean Harlow's manicurist. 7000 Romaine looks itself like a faded movie exterior, a pastel building with chipped *art moderne* detailing, the windows now either boarded or paned with chicken-wire glass and, at the entrance, among the dusty oleander, a rubber mat that reads WELCOME.
>
> Actually no one is welcome, for 7000 Romaine belongs to Howard Hughes, and the door is locked. That the Hughes "communications center" should lie here in the dull sunlight of Hammett-Chandler country is one of those circumstances that satisfy one's suspicion that life is indeed a scenario, for the Hughes empire has been in our time the only industrial complex in the world—involving, over the years, machinery manufacture, foreign oil-tool subsidiaries, a brewery, two airlines, immense real-estate holdings, a major motion-picture studio, and an electronics and missile opera-

tion—run by a man whose *modus operandi* most closely resembles that of a character in *The Big Sleep*.

As it happens, I live not far from 7000 Romaine, and I make a point of driving past it every now and then, I suppose in the same spirit that Arthurian scholars visit the Cornish coast. I am interested in the folklore of Howard Hughes . . .

What is pulling us into this article—toward, we hope, some glimpse of how Hughes operates, some hint of the riddle of the Sphinx—is the steady accretion of facts that have pathos and faded glamour. Knowing Jean Harlow's manicurist is such a minimal link to glory, the unwelcoming welcome mat such a queer relic of a golden age when Hollywood's windows weren't paned with chicken-wire glass and the roost was ruled by giants like Mayer and De Mille and Zanuck who could actually be seen exercising their mighty power. We want to know more; we read on.

Another writer whose leads I admire is Garry Wills. Almost every chapter in his *Nixon Agonistes*, for instance, which originated as a series of magazine articles, begins with an arrangement of sentences that dazzle me with their gathering momentum and mordant truth:

> Spiro Agnew's career has about it a somnambulistic surefootedness, an inevitability of advance, that reminds one of Mencken's Coolidge, of the juggernaut of snooze. In an election-eve TV broadcast, Hubert Humphrey proudly displayed Ed Muskie, his monkish second-string Eugene McCarthy. Nixon, on the same night, sat alone, remasticating answers for Bud Wilkinson, his kept TV interrogator. No Agnew in sight. It was said that Nixon regretted his choice, his deal with Thurmond. But Agnew was a guided missile, swung into place, aimed, activated, launched with the minute calculation that marks Nixon. Once the missile was fired,

the less attention it drew to itself the better—like a tor-
pedo churning quiet toward its goal. Agnew has a neck-
less, lidded flow to him, with wraparound hair, a
tubular perfection to his suits or golf outfits, quiet bur-
bling oratory. Subaquatic. He was almost out of sight by
campaign's end; but a good sonar system could hear him
burrowing ahead, on course.

It's a fine lead, doing its job with precise detail, unexpected imagery and words as surprising as a rare bird. Wills
is holding his reader in a tight grip but never patronizing
him.

Another quality I like in a lead is a feeling of enjoyment.
In the following piece Mark Singer, a writer for *The New
Yorker*, lets you know from the start that he had a good time
with this material and expects you to enjoy it as much as he
did. What could be a more pleasant invitation? One of
Singer's strengths is a sense of humor that turns up countless
details that amuse him. But what makes his humor work is
control. He gives the reader the same experience that he
had: being surprised by an entertaining fact. He doesn't
spoil it by pointing out that it's entertaining.

In all sorts of circumstances, people in Brooklyn will
commit murder. This fact fascinates Benjamin Shine
more than it appalls him. Shine is a peaceable gen-
tleman from Borough Park who would hate to be asked
which he prefers—a sunny afternoon stroll alongside
the Belt Parkway with his wife, Tillie, or a dukes-up
double-murder trial. He is a self-taught student of the
behavior of criminals, innocents, witnesses, lawyers,
judges and jurors. He is a court buff. Most weekdays, a
dozen or more buffs show up at the State Supreme
Court Building on Cadman Plaza, in downtown
Brooklyn. Shine attends as regularly as any back-seat
jurisconsult in the borough.

Although Shine has lived in Brooklyn for most of his seventy-three years, he is no provincial. He acknowledges that the other boroughs of New York City have bred their own miscreants. Having spent the past dozen years watching criminal trials in Brooklyn, however, he has found it sensible and convenient to become a specialist. Consequently, he takes more interest in a corpse that has been deposited in an airshaft in Flatbush than in one that has turned up in the trunk of an automobile at LaGuardia Airport or in a vacant lot near Hunt's Point. Shine realizes that in addition to murderers there are anti-social types out there who have the capacity for rape, theft, burglary, kidnapping, arson or aimless mayhem—at times, of course, overlapping occurs—but he devotes most of his attention to homicides. He is not ghoulish, merely curious. "Where there's murder," he often says, quite accurately, "you know something's doing."

And yet there can be no fixed rules for how to write a lead. Within the broad principle of not letting the reader get away, every writer must approach his subject in a manner that most naturally suits what he is writing about and who he is. In proof of which, I'll close with the lead of an article on rugby written by Richard Burton, the actor. Its second sentence is one of the longest I've ever seen, but it is under control all the way. Besides, it sounds very Welsh, and if that's how Welshmen talk it's how they ought to write:

It's difficult for me to know where to start with rugby. I come from a fanatically rugby-conscious Welsh miner's family, know so much about it, have read so much about it, have heard with delight so many massive lies and stupendous exaggerations about it and have contributed my own fair share, and five of my six brothers played it, one with some distinction, and I mean I even knew a

Welsh woman from Taibach who before a home match
at Aberavon would drop goals from around 40 yards
with either foot to entertain the crowd, and her name, I
remember, was Annie Mort and she wore sturdy shoes,
the kind one reads about in books as "sensible," though
the recipient of a kick from one of Annie's shoes would
have been not so much sensible as insensible, and I
even knew a chap called Five-Cush Cannon who won
the sixth replay of a cup final (the previous five encounters having ended with the scores 0–0, 0–0, 0–0, 0–0,
0–0, including extra time) by throwing the ball over the
bar from a scrum 10 yards out in a deep fog and claim-
ing a dropped goal. And getting it.

11. The Ending

After so many words suggesting how to get started I should add a few on how to stop. Knowing when to end an article is far more important than most writers realize. In fact, you should give as much thought to choosing your last sentence as you did to your first. Well, almost as much.

This may seem ridiculous. If the reader has stuck with you from the beginning, trailing you around blind .corners and over bumpy terrain, surely he won't leave when the end is in sight. But he will—because the end that's in sight often turns out to be a mirage. Like the minister's sermon that builds to a series of perfect conclusions that never conclude, an article that doesn't stop at its proper stopping place is suddenly a drag and therefore, ultimately, a failure.

We are most of us still prisoners of the lesson pounded into us by the composition teachers of our youth: that every story must have a beginning, a middle and an end. We can still visualize the outline, with its Roman numerals (I, II and III), which staked out the road we would faithfully trudge, and its sub-numerals (IIa and IIb) denoting lesser paths down which we would briefly poke. But we always promised to get back to III and summarize our journey.

This is all right for elementary and high school students uncertain of their ground. It forces them to see that every piece of writing should have a logical design that introduces and develops a theme. It's a lesson worth knowing at any age—even the professional writer is adrift more often than he would like to admit. But if you are going to write good nonfiction, you must wriggle out of III's dread grip.

You will know you have arrived at III when you see emerging from your typewriter a sentence that begins, "In sum, therefore, it can be noted that . . ." Or a question that asks, "What insights, then, have we been able to glean from . . .?" These are signals to the reader that you are about to repeat in compressed form what you have already told him in detail. His interest begins to falter; the tension that you have built begins to sag.

Yet you will be true to Miss Potter, your teacher, who made you swear eternal fealty to the holy outline. You remind the reader of what can, in sum, therefore, be noted. You go gleaning one more time in insights that you have already adduced.

But the reader hears the laborious sound of cranking. He sees what you are doing and how bored you are by it. He feels the stirrings of resentment. Why didn't you give more thought to how you were going to wind this thing up? Or are you summarizing because you think he's too dumb to get the point? Still, you keep cranking. But the reader has another option. He quits.

This is the negative reason for realizing the importance of the last sentence. Failure to know where that sentence should occur—and what it should consist of—can wreck an article which until its final stage has been tightly constructed.

The positive reason for ending well is not just to avoid ending badly, but because a good last sentence—or paragraph—is a joy in itself. It has its own virtues, which give the reader a lift and which linger when the article is over.

The perfect ending should take the reader slightly by surprise and yet seem exactly right to him. He didn't expect the article to end so soon, or so abruptly, or to say what it said.

But he knows it when he sees it. Like a good lead, it works. It's like the curtain line in a theatrical comedy. We are in the middle of a scene (we think) when suddenly one of the actors says something funny, or outrageous, or epigrammatic, and the lights go out. We are momentarily startled to find the scene over, and then delighted by the aptness of how it ended. What delights us, subconsciously, is the playwright's perfect control.

For the nonfiction writer, the simplest way of putting this into a rule is: When you're ready to stop, stop. If you have presented all the facts and made the point that you want to make, look for the nearest exit.

Often it takes just a few sentences to get out of the article in the same style that you used to get in. Going back to Garry Wills' *Nixon Agonistes*, here's how he ends the chapter on "Ted" Agnew, whom we last saw launched missile-like, sub-aquatic, into the political ocean of American life:

> There is a difference between ambition and opportunism. Leisurely "Ted" is not driven by Nixon's demons. He does not knock himself out; he does not even do his homework. But he is opportunistic—not cynically so; when lucky breaks come, one takes them, grateful. Man's function is to reap the fruits of our beneficent system. How foolish of "the kids" not to understand this. As he told them in the campaign: "You may give us your symptoms; we will make the diagnosis and we, the Establishment, will implement the cure." It is a message that he did not try to take to Miami's blacks.

The blunt irony of that final sentence brings echoes of Mencken rumbling down the decades again, as so often happens for me when one of America's bleakest truths is seen through a glass plainly. Here is how Mencken ends his appraisal of Coolidge, whose appeal to the "customers" was that his "government governed hardly at all; thus the ideal of

Jefferson was realized at last, and the Jeffersonians were delighted":

> We suffer most, not when the White House is a
> peaceful dormitory, but when it [has] a tin-pot Paul
> bawling from the roof. Counting out Harding as a cipher
> only, Dr. Coolidge was preceded by one World Saver
> and followed by two more. What enlightened American,
> having to choose between any of them and another
> Coolidge, would hesitate for an instant? There were no
> thrills while he reigned, but neither were there any
> headaches. He had no ideas, and he was not a nuisance.

These are the elements to look for when instinct tells you
it's time to stop. Both the Agnew sentence and the Coolidge
sentence send the reader on his way quickly and with a provocative thought to take along. The notion of Coolidge having no ideas and not being a nuisance is bound to leave a
residue of enjoyment. It works.

But what often works best is a quotation. Try to find in
your notes some remark that has a sense of finality, or that's
funny, or that adds an unexpected last detail. Sometimes it
will jump out at you in the process of writing. Put it aside
and save it. If the remark doesn't jump out, go back and look
for it among all the things said or written by anyone mentioned in the article.

In the mid-1960s, when Woody Allen was just becoming
established as America's resident neurotic, still mainly doing
nightclub monologues, I wrote the first long magazine piece
that took note of his arrival. It ended like this:

> "If people come away relating to me as a person," Al-
> len says, "rather than just enjoying my jokes; if they
> come away wanting to hear me again, no matter what I
> might talk about, then I'm succeeding." Judging by the
> returns, he is. Woody Allen is Mr. Related-To, Mr. Pop

Therapy, and he seems a good bet to hold the franchise for many years.

Yet he does have a problem all his own, unshared by, unrelated to, the rest of America. "I'm obsessed," he says, "by the fact that my mother genuinely resembles Groucho Marx."

There's a remark from so far out in left field that nobody could see it coming. The surprise that it carries is tremendous. How could it not be a perfect ending?

Surprise is one of the most refreshing commodities in writing. If something surprises you, it will almost surely surprise—and delight—the people you are writing for.

12. The Interview

Get people talking. Learn to ask questions that will elicit answers about what is most interesting or vivid in their lives. Nothing so animates writing as someone telling what he thinks or what he does—in his own words.

His own words will always be better than your words, even if you are the most elegant stylist in the land. They carry the inflection of his speaking voice and the idiosyncrasies of how he puts a sentence together. They contain the regionalisms of his conversation and the lingo of his trade. They convey his enthusiasms. This is a person talking to the reader directly, not through the filter of a writer. As soon as a writer steps in, everybody else's experience becomes secondhand.

Therefore learn how to conduct an interview. Whatever form of nonfiction you write, it will come alive in proportion to the number of "quotes" you can weave into it naturally as you go along. Often, in fact, you will find yourself embarking on an article so apparently lifeless—the history of an institution, perhaps, or some local issue such as storm sewers—that you will quail at the prospect of keeping your readers, or even yourself, awake.

Take heart. You will find the solution if you look for the human element. Somewhere in every drab institution are men and women who have a fierce attachment to what they are doing and are rich repositories of lore. Somewhere behind every storm sewer is a politician whose future hangs on getting it installed and a widow who has always lived on the block and is outraged that some damn-fool legislator thinks it will wash away. Find these people to tell your story and it won't be drab.

I have proved this to myself many times. In 1961 I agreed to write a small book for the New York Public Library to celebrate the fiftieth anniversary of its main building on Fifth Avenue. On the surface it seemed to be just the story of a marble building and millions of musty volumes. But behind the façade I found that the Library had nineteen research divisions, each with a curator supervising a hoard of treasures and oddities, from Washington's handwritten Farewell Address to 750,000 movie stills. I decided to interview all these curators to learn what was in their collections, what they were adding to keep up with new areas of knowledge, and how their rooms were being used.

I found, for instance, that the Science and Technology division had a collection of patents second only to that of the United States Patent Office and was therefore almost a second home to the city's patent lawyers. But it also had a daily stream of men and women who obviously thought they were on the verge of discovering perpetual motion. "Everybody's got something to invent," the curator explained, "but they won't tell us what they're looking for—maybe because they think we'll patent it ourselves." The whole building turned out to be just such a mixture of scholars and searchers and crackpots, and my story, though ostensibly the chronicle of an institution, was really a story about people.

I used the same approach in a long article about Sotheby's, the thriving London auction firm. Sotheby's was also divided into various domains, such as silver and porcelain and art, each with an expert in charge, and, like the Library, it subsisted on the whims of a capricious public. The experts were like department heads in a small college, and all of them had anecdotes that were unique both in substance and in the manner of telling:

"We just sit here like Micawber waiting for things to come in," said R. S. Timewell, head of the furniture department. "Recently an old lady near Cambridge wrote that she wanted to raise two thousand pounds and asked if I would go through her house and see if her furniture would fetch that much. I did, and there was absolutely nothing of value. As I was about to leave I said, 'Have I seen *every* thing?' She said I had, except for a maid's room that she hadn't bothered to show me. The room had a very fine 18th-century chest that the old lady was using to store blankets in. 'Your worries are over,' I told her, 'if you sell that chest.' She said, 'But that's quite impossible—where will I store my blankets?'"

My worries were over, too. By listening to the quizzical scholars who ran the business and to the men and women who flocked there every morning bearing unloved objects found in British attics ("I'm afraid it *isn't* Queen Anne, Madam—much nearer Queen Victoria, unfortunately") I got as much human detail as a writer could want.

Finally, when I was asked in 1966 to write a history of the Book-of-the-Month Club to mark its fortieth birthday, I thought I might encounter nothing but inert matter. But again I found a peppery human element on both sides of the fence, for the books had always been selected by a panel of strong-minded judges and sent to equally stubborn subscribers, who never hesitated to wrap up a book they didn't like and send it right back.

I was given more than 1,000 pages of transcribed interviews with the five original judges (Heywood Broun, Henry Seidel Canby, Dorothy Canfield, Christopher Morley and William Allen White), to which I added my own interviews with the Club's founder, Harry Scherman, and with the judges who were then active. The result was four decades' worth of personal memories on how America's reading tastes had changed, and why, and even the books took on a life of their own and became characters in my story:

"Probably it's difficult for anyone who remembers the prodigious success of *Gone With the Wind*," Dorothy Canfield said, "to think how it would have seemed to people who encountered it simply as a very, very long and detailed book about the Civil War and its aftermath. We had never heard of the author and didn't have anybody else's opinion on it. It was chosen with a little difficulty, because some of the characterization was not very authentic or convincing. But as a narrative it had the quality which the French call *attention:* it made you want to turn over the page to see what happens next. I remember that someone commented, 'Well, people may not like it very much, but nobody can deny that it gives a lot of reading for your money.' Its tremendous success was, I must say, about as surprising to us as to anybody else."

These three examples are typical of the kind of information that is locked inside people's heads which a good nonfiction writer must unlock. The best way to practice is to go out and interview people. The interview itself is one of the most common and popular nonfiction forms, so you might as well master it early.

How should you start? First, decide what person you want to interview. If you are a college student, don't interview your roommate. With all due respect for what a fine fellow he is, he probably doesn't have much to say that the rest of us want to hear. To learn the craft of nonfiction you must push yourself out into the real world—your town or your city or your county—and pretend that you're writing for a real publication. If it helps, decide which publication you are hypothetically writing for. In any case, choose as your subject someone whose job is so important, or interesting, or unusual, that the average reader would want to read about him.

This doesn't mean that he has to be president of General Motors. He can be the owner of the local pizza parlor or supermarket or hairdressing academy. He can be the fisherman who puts out to sea every morning, or the Little League manager, or the cop. He can be the butcher, the baker or—better yet, if you can find him—the candlestick maker. Look for the women in your community who are unraveling the old myths about what the two sexes were foreordained to do. Choose, in short, someone who touches some corner of the reader's life.

Interviewing is one of those skills that you can only get better at. You will never again feel so ill at ease as when you try it for the first time, and probably you'll never feel entirely comfortable prodding another person for answers that he or she may be too shy to reveal, or too inarticulate. But at least half of the skill is mechanical. The rest is instinct— knowing how to make the other person relax, when to push, when to listen, when to stop. And this can all be learned with experience.

The basic tools for an interview are paper and two or three well-sharpened pencils. Is that the most insultingly obvious advice? You'd be surprised how many writers venture forth to stalk their quarry with no pencil, or with one that breaks, or with a pen that doesn't work, and with nothing to write on. "Be prepared" is as apt a motto for the nonfiction writer on his mundane rounds as it is for the Boy Scout alert for the traditional old lady trying to cross the street.

But keep your notebook or paper out of sight until you need it. There's nothing less likely to relax a person than the arrival of someone with a stenographer's pad. Both of you need time to get to know each other. Take a while just to chat, gauging what sort of person you're dealing with, getting him or her to trust you.

Never go into an interview without doing whatever homework you can. If you are interviewing a town official, know his voting record. If it's an actor, know what plays he has been in. You will be resented if you inquire about facts that you could have learned in advance.

Make a list of likely questions—it will save you the vast embarrassment of going dry in mid-interview. Perhaps you won't need it; better questions will occur to you, or the person being interviewed will veer off at an angle you couldn't have foreseen. Here you can only go by intuition. If he strays hopelessly off the subject, drag him back. If you like the new direction, follow him and forget the questions you intended to ask.

Many beginning interviewers are crippled by the fear that they are imposing on the other person and have no right to invade his privacy. This fear is almost 100 percent unfounded. Unless the other person is a Howard Hughes, he is delighted that somebody wants to interview him. Most men and women lead lives, if not of quiet desperation, at least of desperate quietness, and they jump at a chance to talk about their work to an outsider who seems eager to listen.

This doesn't necessarily mean that it will go well. In general you will be talking to people who have never been interviewed before, and they will warm to the process awkwardly, self-consciously, perhaps not giving you anything that you can use. Come back another day; it will go better. You will both even begin to enjoy it—proof that you aren't forcing your victim to do something he doesn't really want to do.

Speaking of tools, you will ask if it's all right to use a tape recorder. Why not just take one along, start it going, and forget all that business of pencil and paper?

Obviously the tape recorder is a superb instrument for capturing what people have to say—especially people who, for reasons of their culture or education or temperament, would never get around to writing it down. In this realm of social anthropology the machine is literally invaluable. I admire the books of Studs Terkel, which he "wrote" by recording long interviews with ordinary people and stitching the results into coherent shape. I also like the question-and-answer interviews, obtained by tape recorder, that have long been published in *Playboy*. They have the sound of spontaneity and the refreshing absence of a writer hovering over the product and burnishing it to a high gloss.

But, strictly, this isn't writing. It's a process of asking questions and then pruning and splicing the answers, and it takes endless time and care and labor. People who seem to be talking into the tape recorder with linear precision and economy turn out, when the interview is transcribed, to have been stumbling so aimlessly over the sands of grammar that they haven't completed a single decent sentence. Hence my admiration for Terkel and other stewards of the spoken word. The seemingly simple use of a tape recorder isn't simple.

My main reasons for warning you off it, however, are practical ones. The various hazards hardly need to be mentioned. One is that you don't usually have a tape recorder with you—you are more apt to have a pencil. Another is that tape recorders malfunction. Few moments in journalism are as glum as the return of a reporter with "a really great story," followed by his pushing of the Play button and total silence. But, above all, a writer should be able to see his materials. If your interview is on tape you become a listener, forever fussing with the machine, running it backward to find a brilliant remark that you can never quite find, running it forward, stopping, starting, driving yourself crazy. Be a writer. Write things down.

Still, taking notes has one big problem. The person you're interviewing often starts talking faster than you can write. You are still scribbling Sentence A when he zooms into Sentence B. You drop Sentence A and pursue him into Sentence B, meanwhile trying to hold the rest of Sentence A in your inner ear and hoping that Sentence C will be a dud that you can skip altogether, using the time to catch up. Unfortunately, you now have your man going at high speed. He is at last saying all the things you have been trying to cajole out of him for an hour, and saying them with what seems to be Churchillian eloquence. Your inner ear is clogging up with sentences that you want to grab before they slip away.

Tell him to stop. Just say, "Hold it a minute, please," and write until you catch up. What you are trying to do with your feverish scribbling, after all, is to quote him correctly, and nobody wants to be misquoted.

With practice you will write faster and develop some form of shorthand. You'll find yourself devising abbreviations for often-used words and also omitting the small connective syntax. As soon as the interview is over, fill in all the missing words that you can remember. Complete the uncompleted sentences. Most of them will still be lingering just within the bounds of recall.

When you get home, type out your notes—now an almost illegible scrawl—so that you can read them easily. This not only makes the interview accessible, along with any clippings or other materials you may have assembled. It enables you to review in tranquillity a torrent of words that you wrote in haste, and thereby discover what the person really said.

You will find that he said much that is redundant or dull. Try to single out the quotations that are most important or colorful. You will be tempted to use all the words that are in your notes because you performed the laborious chore of getting all the words down. But this is no reason to put the reader to the same trouble. Your job is to distill the essence.

What about your obligation to the person you interviewed? To what extent can you cut or juggle his words? This question vexes every writer returning from his first interview—and it should. But the answer is not hard if you keep in mind two standards: brevity and fair play.

Your ethical duty to the person being interviewed is to present his position accurately. If he carefully weighed two sides of an issue and you only quote his views of one side, making him seem to favor that position, you will misrepresent what he told you. Or you might misrepresent him by quoting him out of context, or by choosing only some flashy remark without adding the serious afterthought. You are dealing with a man's honor and reputation—and also with your own.

But after that your duty is to the reader. He deserves the smallest package. Most people meander in their conversation, filling it with irrelevant tales and trivia. Much of it is delightful, but it is still trivia. Your interview will be strong to the extent that you get the main points made without waste.

Therefore if you find on page 5 of your notes a comment that perfectly amplifies a point on page 2—a point made earlier in the interview—you will do everyone a favor if you link the two thoughts, letting the second sentence follow and illustrate the first. This may violate the truth of how the interview progressed, but you will be true to the intent of what was said. Play with the "quotes" by all means—selecting, rejecting, thinning, transposing their order, saving a good one for the end. Just make sure that the play is fair. Don't change any words or let the cutting of a sentence distort the proper context of what remains.

Do I literally mean "don't change any words"? Yes and no. If a speaker chooses his words carefully, there's no excuse for not quoting him verbatim. Most interviewers are quite sloppy about this; they think that if they achieve a rough approximation it's good enough. It's not good enough: nobody wants to see himself in print using words he wouldn't ever use. But if the speaker's conversation is ragged—if his sentences trail off, if his thoughts are disjointed, if his syntax is so tangled that it would embarrass him—the writer has no choice but to clean up the English and provide the missing links.

Sometimes, in fact, you can fall into a curious trap in your effort to be true to the speaker. As you write your article, you type his words exactly as you took them down. You even allow yourself a moment of satisfaction at being such a faithful scribe. Later, editing what you've written, you realize that several of the quotes don't quite make sense. When you first heard them, they sounded so felicitous that you didn't give them a second thought. Now, on second thought, there's a hole somewhere in the language or the logic. To leave the hole is no favor to the reader or the speaker—and no credit to the writer. You have to patch the damage. Often you only need to add one or two clarifying words. Or you might find another quote in your notes that makes the same point—speakers tend to be repetitive. But don't forget that you can always call the person you interviewed. Tell him you want to check a few of the things he said. Get him to rephrase his points until they're clear. Don't ever let yourself become the prisoner of your quotes—so lulled by how wonderful they sound that you never stop to analyze them.

As for how to organize the interview, every one is different, so I will leave you to discern its logical shape and will only add a few technical hints.

The lead obviously should tell the reader, like all leads, why the person is worth reading about. What is his claim to our time and attention? Thereafter, try to achieve a balance between what the subject is saying in *his* words and what you are writing in *your* words to explain and to connect. If you quote a person for three or four consecutive paragraphs, this becomes monotonous. Quotations are livelier when you break them up, making periodic appearances in your role as guide. You are still the writer—don't relinquish control. But make your appearances useful; don't just insert one of those dreary sentences which shout to the reader that your sole purpose is to break up a string of quotations ("He stopped and tapped his pipe on a nearby ashtray and I noticed that his fingers were quite long").

When you use a quotation, start the sentence with it. Don't lead up to it with a vapid phrase saying what the man said.

> GOOD: "I usually like to go downtown once a week," Mr. Smith said, "and have lunch with some of my old friends."
> BAD: Mr. Smith said that he liked to "go downtown once a week and have lunch with some of my old friends."

The first sentence has vitality, the second is dead. In fact, nothing is deader than to start a sentence with a "Mr. Smith said" construction—it's where countless readers stop reading. If the man said it, let him say it and get the sentence off to a warm, human start.

But be careful where you break the quotation. Do it as soon as you naturally can, so that the reader knows who is talking, but not where it will destroy the rhythm or the sense. Notice how the following three variants all inflict some kind of damage:

> "I usually like," Mr. Smith said, "to go downtown once a week and have lunch with some of my old friends."
> "I usually like to go downtown," Mr. Smith said,

"once a week and have lunch with some of my old
friends."

"I usually like to go downtown once a week and have
lunch," Mr. Smith said, "with some of my old friends."

Finally, don't strain to find synonyms for "he said." Don't
make your man assert, aver and expostulate just to avoid
repeating "he said," and please—please!—don't write "he
smiled" or "he grinned." I have never heard anybody smile.
The reader's eye skips over "he said" anyway, so it's not
worth a lot of fuss. If you crave variety, choose synonyms
that catch the shifting nature of the conversation. "He
pointed out," "he explained," "he replied," "he added"—
these all carry a particular meaning. But don't use "he
added" if the man is merely averring and not putting a
postscript on what he just said.

I'll close by adding as a postscript a passage from *The Bottom of the Harbor,* by Joseph Mitchell, my own favorite
writer of long nonfiction articles. The book consists of various articles that Mitchell wrote for *The New Yorker* about
people who live and work around the waterfront. One reason
I admire Joseph Mitchell is that he is a master of the uncom-
monly difficult art of writing about the so-called common
man without ever patronizing him.

This is part of an interview with the captain of a fishing
boat called a "dragger" that operates out of Stonington, Connecticut. Note the deceptively simple style, the exactness of
detail and especially the deft interweaving of Mitchell's
words with those of the captain, Ellery Thompson:

Ellery is a self-taught B-flat trumpet player. While
living on the *Eleanor,* he spent many evenings in the
cabin by himself practicing hymns and patriotic music.
Sometimes, out on the grounds, if he had a few minutes
to kill, he would go below and practice. One afternoon,
blundering around the Hell Hole in a thick summer fog,

he grew tired of cranking the foghorn and got out his trumpet and stood on deck and played "The Star-Spangled Banner" over and over, alarming the crews of other draggers fogbound in the area, who thought an excursion boat was bearing down on them. After he went back to sleeping at home, he continued to practice in the evenings, but he had to give it up before long because of its effect on his mother's health.

"At that time," he says, "I was working hard on three hymns—'Up from the Grave He Arose,' 'There Is a Fountain Filled with Blood' and 'What a Friend We Have in Jesus.' I had 'What a Friend' just about where I wanted it. One evening after supper, I went in the parlor as usual and Ma was sitting on the settee reading the *Ladies' Home Journal* and I took the easy chair and went to work on 'What a Friend.' I was running through it the second or third time when, all of a sudden, Ma bust out crying. I laid my trumpet down and I asked her what in the world was the matter. 'That trumpet's what's the matter,' Ma said. 'It makes me sad.' She said it made her so sad she was having nightmares and losing weight."

Ellery walks with a pronounced stoop, favoring his left shoulder, where the rheumatism has settled, and he takes his time. "If I start to hustle and bustle," he says, "everything I eat repeats and repeats." He abhors hurry; he thinks that humanity in general has got ahead of itself. He once threatened to fire a man in his crew because he worked too hard. . . .

Ellery is about as self-sufficient as a man can be. He has no wife, no politics and no religion. "I put off getting married until I got me a good big boat," he says. "When I got the boat and got it paid for, the Depression struck. There's mighty few women that'll eat fish three times a day, and that's about all I had to offer. I kept putting it off until times got better. When times got better, I got the rheumatism. And a man in his middle forties with the chronic rheumatism, there's not much of the old Romeo left in him."

Ellery is a member of only one organization. "I'm a Mason," he says. "Aside from that, the only thing I belong to is the human race." His father was a Republican and his mother is a Democrat; he says he has never put any dependence in either party and has never once voted for anybody. His family belongs to the Baptist Church; he says he has somehow managed to get along without it. "I enjoy hymns," he says. "I enjoy the old ones, the gloomy ones. I used to go to church just to hear the good old hymns, but the sermons finally drove me away."

13. Writing About a Place

Next to knowing how to write about people, you should know how to write about a place. People and places are the twin pillars on which most nonfiction is built. Every human event happens somewhere, and the reader wants to know what that "somewhere" was like.

In a few cases you'll need only a paragraph or two to sketch the setting of an event. But more often you'll need to evoke the mood of a whole neighborhood or town to give texture to the story you are telling. And in certain cases, such as the travel piece itself—that perennial form in which you recount how you lived on a houseboat in Kashmir or crossed the Sahara by bus—descriptive detail will be the main substance.

Whatever the proportion, it would seem to be relatively easy. The dismal truth is that it's very hard. It must be hard, because it's in this area that most writers—professional and amateur—produce not only their worst work, but work that is just plain terrible. The terrible work has nothing to do with some terrible flaw of character. On the contrary, it results from the virtue of enthusiasm. Nobody turns so quickly into a bore as a traveler home from his travels. He enjoyed his trip so much that he wants to tell us all about it—and "all" is what we don't want to hear. We only want to hear some. What made his trip different from everybody else's? What can he tell us that we don't already know? We don't

want him to describe every ride at Disneyland, or tell us
that the Grand Canyon is awesome, or that Venice has ca-
nals. If one of the rides at Disneyland got stuck, or if somebody fell into the awesome Grand Canyon, *that* would be
worth hearing about.

It's natural for all of us when we have gone to a certain
place to feel that somehow we are the first people who ever
went there or thought such sensitive thoughts about it. Fair
enough—it's what keeps us going and validates our experience. Who can visit the Tower of London without musing on
the wives of Henry VIII, or visit Egypt and not be moved by
the size and antiquity of the pyramids?

But this is ground already covered by many people. As a
writer you must keep a tight rein on your subjective self—
the traveler touched by new sights and sounds and smells—
and keep an objective eye on the reader. The article that
records what you did every day on your trip will fascinate
you because it was your trip. Will it fascinate the reader?
Nine times out of ten it won't. The mere agglomeration of
detail is no free pass to his interest. The detail must in some
way be significant.

The other big trap is style. Nowhere else in nonfiction do
writers use such syrupy words and groaning platitudes. Adjectives that you would squirm to use in conversation—
"roseate," "wondrous," "fabled"—are common currency.
Half the sights seen in a day's sightseeing are "quaint," especially windmills and covered bridges. They are certified for
quaintness.

It is a style of soft words which under hard examination
mean nothing, or which mean different things to different
people: "attractive," "charming," "romantic." To write that
"the city has its own attractiveness" is no help—every city
does. And who will define "charm," except possibly the
owner of a charm school? Or "romantic"? These are subjec-

tive concepts in the eye of the beholder. One man's romantic sunrise is another man's hangover.

Travelese is a land "where old meets new." I'm amazed at the number of places where old meets new. Old never meets old. The meeting occurs in the "twisting alleys" and "bustling thoroughfares" of storied Tangier or picturesque Zanzibar. This is terrain dotted with "byways," usually half-forgotten or at least hidden. It's a world where inanimate objects spring to transitive life: storefronts smile, buildings boast, ruins beckon and the very chimney tops sing their immemorial song of welcome. The clichés bloom with very fertility.

How can you overcome such fearful odds and write well about a place? My advice can be reduced to two principles— one of style, the other of substance.

First, choose your words with unusual care. If a phrase comes to you easily, look at it with deep suspicion—it's probably one of the innumerable clichés that have woven their way so tightly into the fabric of travel writing that it takes a special effort *not* to use them. Also resist straining for the luminous lyrical phrase to describe the wondrous waterfall. At best it will make you sound artificial—unlike yourself—and at worst pompous. Strive for fresh words and images. Leave "myriad" and their ilk to the poets. Leave "ilk" to anyone who will take it away.

As for substance, be intensely selective. If you are describing a beach, don't write that "the shore was scattered with rocks" or that "occasionally a seagull flew over." Shores have a tendency to be scattered with rocks and to be flown over by seagulls. Eliminate every such fact that is a known attribute: don't tell us that the sea had waves and the sand was white. Find details that are significant. They may be important to your narrative; they may be unusual, or colorful, or comic, or entertaining. But make sure they are details that do useful work.

I'll give you some examples from various writers, widely
different in temperament but alike in the effectiveness of the
detail they chose. The first is from an article by Joan Didion
called "Some Dreamers of the Golden Dream." It's about a
lurid crime that occurred in the San Bernardino Valley of
California, and in this early passage the writer is taking us,
as if in her own car, away from urban civilization to the
lonely stretch of road where Lucille Miller's Volkswagen so
unaccountably caught fire:

> This is the California where it is easy to Dial-A-Devo-
> tion, but hard to buy a book. This is the country of the
> teased hair and the Capris and the girls for whom all
> life's promise comes down to a waltz-length white wed-
> ding dress and the birth of a Kimberly or a Sherry or a
> Debbi and a Tijuana divorce and a return to hair-
> dressers' school. "We were just crazy kids," they say
> without regret, and look to the future. The future al-
> ways looks good in the golden land, because no one re-
> members the past. Here is where the hot wind blows
> and the old ways do not seem relevant, where the di-
> vorce rate is double the national average and where one
> person in every 38 lives in a trailer. Here is the last stop
> for all those who come from somewhere else, for all
> those who drifted away from the cold and the past and
> the old ways. Here is where they are trying to find a
> new life style, trying to find it in the only places they
> know to look: the movies and the newspapers. The case
> of Lucille Marie Maxwell Miller is a tabloid monument
> to the new style.
>
> Imagine Banyan Street first, because Banyan is where
> it happened. The way to Banyan is to drive west from
> San Bernardino out Foothill Boulevard, Route 66: past
> the Santa Fe switching yards, the Forty Winks Motel.
> Past the motel that is 19 stucco tepees: "SLEEP IN A

WIGWAM—GET MORE FOR YOUR WAMPUM." Past Fontana Drag City and Fontana Church of the Nazarene and the Pit Stop A Go-Go; past Kaiser Steel, through Cucamonga, out to the Kapu Kai Restaurant-Bar and Coffee Shop, at the corner of Route 66 and Carnelian Avenue. Up Carnelian Avenue from the Kapu Kai, which means "Forbidden Seas," the subdivision flags whip in the harsh wind. "HALF-ACRE RANCHES! SNACK BARS! TRAVERTINE ENTRIES! $95 DOWN." It is the trail of an intention gone haywire, the flotsam of the New California. But after a while the signs thin out on Carnelian Avenue, and the houses are no longer the bright pastels of the Springtime Home owners but the faded bungalows of the people who grow a few grapes and keep a few chickens out here, and then the hill gets steeper and the road climbs and even the bungalows are few, and here—desolate, roughly surfaced, lined with eucalyptus and lemon groves—is Banyan Street.

In only two paragraphs we have a feeling not only for the tackiness of the New California landscape, with its stucco tepees and instant housing and borrowed Hawaiian romance, but for the pathetic impermanence of the lives and pretensions of the people who have alighted there. All the details—statistics and names and signs—are doing helpful work.

Concrete detail is also the anchor of John McPhee's prose. McPhee has written well over a dozen books since 1964, each one different in subject, each a model of craftsmanship. *Coming into the Country*, his book about Alaska, has a section devoted to the quest for a possible new state capital. It takes him only a few sentences to give us a sense of what's wrong with the present capital, both as a place to live and as a place for lawmakers to make good laws:

A pedestrian today in Juneau, head down and charging, can be stopped for no gain by the wind. There are railings along the streets by which senators and representatives can haul themselves to work. Over the past couple of years, a succession of wind gauges were placed on a ridge above the town. They could measure velocities up to 200 miles per hour. They did not survive. The taku winds tore them apart after driving their indicators to the end of the scale. The weather is not always so bad; but under its influence the town took shape, and so Juneau is a tight community of adjacent buildings and narrow European streets, adhering to its mountainsides and fronting the salt water. . . .

The urge to move the capital came over Harris during those two years [in the Alaska State Senate]. Sessions began in January and ran on at least three months, and Harris developed what he called "a complete sense of isolation—stuck there. People couldn't get at you. You were in a cage. You talked to the hard lobbyists every day. Every day the same people. What was going on needed more airing."

The oddity of the city, so remote from the ordinary American experience, is instantly clear. One possibility for the legislators was to move the capital to Anchorage. There at least nobody would feel that he was in an alien town. McPhee distills its essence in a paragraph that is brilliant both in detail and in metaphor:

Almost all Americans would recognize Anchorage, because Anchorage is that part of any city where the city has burst its seams and extruded Colonel Sanders. Anchorage is sometimes excused in the name of pioneering. Build now, civilize later. But Anchorage is not a frontier town. It is virtually unrelated to its environment. It has come in on the wind, an American spore. A large cookie cutter brought down on El Paso could lift something like Anchorage into the air. Anchorage is the northern rim of Trenton, the center of Oxnard, the ocean-blind precincts of Daytona Beach. It is condensed, instant Albuquerque.

Another kind of travel writing, the personal memoir, a rich form because it taps so many wells of childhood and growing up, also depends on the writer's ability to call back what made his neighborhood distinctive, his early life unique. One of my favorite examples is Alfred Kazin's *A Walker in the City*. The locale is Brownsville, a Jewish ghetto in Brooklyn, and the detail tends to be sensual. Smells, for instance, are evocative for Kazin. For another writer, what stirs a specific memory might be a sound, or the theme song of an old radio show.

Here is a fragment of Kazin's youth:

It was the darkness and emptiness of the streets I liked most about Friday evening, as if in preparation for that day of rest and worship which the Jews greet "as a bride"—that day when the very touch of money is prohibited, all work, all travel, all household duties, even to the turning on and off of a light—Jewry had found its way past its tormented heart to some ancient still center of itself. I waited for the streets to go dark on Friday evening as other children waited for the Christmas lights. . . . When I returned home after three, the warm odor of a coffee cake baking in the oven, and the sight of my mother on her hands and knees scrubbing the linoleum on the dining room floor, filled me with such tenderness that I could feel my senses reaching out to embrace every single object in our household. . . .

My great moment came at six, when my father returned from work, his overalls smelling faintly of turpentine and shellac, white drops of silver paint still gleaming on his chin. Hanging his overcoat in the long dark hall that led into our kitchen, he would leave in one pocket a loosely folded copy of the New York *World;* and then everything that beckoned to me from that other hemisphere of my brain beyond the East River would start up from the smell of fresh newsprint and the sight of the globe on the front page. It was a paper that carried special associations for me with Brooklyn Bridge. They published the *World* under the green dome on Park Row overlooking the bridge; the fresh salt air of New York harbor lingered for me in the smell of paint and damp newsprint in the hall. I felt that my father brought the outside straight into our house with each day's copy.

Another area where your success will rest on freshness of detail is the vast field of exploration and adventure, especially when it also involves the history of an obscure region and the reconstruction of events that happened long ago. For me the best hand at this difficult work is Alan Moorehead. I have followed him across much of Africa and Australia and Asia and the Pacific, always struck with admiration bordering on disbelief that he could collate such a wealth of present and past experience and write about it with seemingly effortless warmth.

His books *The White Nile* and *The Blue Nile* are marvels of craftsmanship. Though they deal with a huge gallery of men and women who sought the source of those rivers in the nineteenth century, bedeviled by hostile nature and hostile tribes, by illness and ignorance, by jurisdictional squabbles in the interior and back home in England, all the characters are wonderfully alive, and so is Moorehead as a writer, stitching his own observations of Africa together with what he has extracted from the journals of the explorers who preceded him up the Nile long ago.

Moorehead's style is so uniformly pleasant that I could quote from almost any page of his books or articles. The following excerpt is as good as any because it is descriptive material of the kind that is ordinarily so susceptible to banalities and purple prose:

Many years have gone by since I first flew up the valley of the upper Nile, starting the journey at Khartoum, in the Sudan, and ending it nearly two thousand miles away, at the source of the river, in Uganda. I was a war correspondent at the time, on my way from one campaign, in the western desert of Egypt, to another, in Ethiopia. Even then, when planes did not fly nearly so high as they do today, there was not very much to be seen from the air except the endless desert and the meandering green line of the river, but there were frequent stops along the way, and these I remember just as distinctly as one remembers the islands on a long ocean voyage.

Before we started, we were held up for three or four days at Khartoum with engine trouble. It was April, the hottest time of the year—so hot, in fact, that it was slightly painful just to touch the porcelain sides of your bathtub when you got up in the morning. A fearsome sandstorm known as a *haboob* was blowing, and it was only at the very end of the long, torpid day that the town woke up at last. Each evening, about an hour before the light began to fail, I used to walk down to the zoo with a book. The Khartoum Zoo is quite unlike any other zoo in the world. It lies on the left bank of the Blue Nile, just upstream from the point where the White Nile comes in from the southern Sudan, and it covers hardly more than two or three acres.

The animals and the birds do not have that vacant and dispirited air that seems to overtake tropical creatures when they are transported to cold climates in the north. They have all been born here in this hothouse atmosphere, and many of them are not kept in cages; they simply roam about in their natural state, grazing on the grass and the bushes or wading in the pond. At the hour when I used to go to the zoo, there were hardly any visitors, and as I sat there reading, the zebras, the antelopes and many kinds of long-legged birds would gather around in a quiet and hesitating way that was something between curiosity and fear. It was very pleasant and very peaceful, and this made it all the more surprising one evening when I looked up from my book and found General de Gaulle standing before me. He was wearing a pale-blue kepi and a tropical uniform, and as I rose from my bench he saluted in a friendly, informal way and went off to see the giraffes. Heaven knows what he was doing in that outlandish place. I saw him only twice more during the war—once at Casablanca, with Roosevelt and Churchill, and then during the Liberation of Paris, when he marched down the Champs-Elysées at the head of his men and we were all in tears.

Finally, let me come to that troublesome organism, the travel piece itself. This is the article whose primary purpose is to describe a certain place—never mind such collateral purposes as telling a story or reconstructing a set of events. Practice writing this kind of article, and just because I call it a travel piece I don't mean that you have to go to Khartoum. Go to your local shopping mall, or bowling alley, or park. Or write about your vacation. But whatever place you write about, go there long enough or often enough to isolate the qualities that make it special. Usually this will be some combination of the place and the people who inhabit it. If it's your local bowling alley it will be a mixture of the atmosphere inside and the regular patrons. If it's a foreign city it will be some mixture of the ancient culture and its present populace. Try to find it.

A master of this feat of detection is the English author V. S. Pritchett, one of the best and most versatile of nonfiction writers. Consider what he squeezes out of a visit to Istanbul:

> Istanbul has meant so much to the imagination that the reality shocks most travelers. We cannot get the sultans out of our minds. We half expect to find them still cross-legged and jewelled on their divans. We remember tales of the harem. The truth is that Istanbul has no glory except its situation. It is a city of steep, cobbled, noisy hills. . . .
>
> Mostly the shops sell cloth, clothes, stockings, shoes, the Greek traders rushing out, with cloth unrolled, at any potential customer, the Turks passively waiting. Porters shout; everyone shouts; you are butted by horses, knocked sideways by loads of bedding, and, through all this, you see one of the miraculous sights of Turkey—a demure youth carrying a brass tray suspended on three chains, and in the exact center of the tray a small glass of red tea. He never spills it; he maneuvers it through chaos to his boss, who is sitting on the doorstep of his shop.
>
> One realizes there are two breeds in Turkey: those who carry and those who sit. No one sits quite so relaxedly, expertly, beatifically as a Turk; he sits with every inch of his body; his very face sits. He sits as if he inherited the art from generations of sultans in the palace above Seraglio Point. Nothing he likes better than to invite you to sit with him in his shop or in his office with half a dozen other sitters: a few polite inquiries about your age, your marriage, the sex of your children, the number of your relations, and where and how you live,

and then, like the other sitters, you clear your throat with a hawk that surpasses anything heard in Lisbon, New York or Sheffield, and join the general silence.

I like the phrase "his very face sits"—just four short words, but they convey an idea so fanciful that they take us by surprise. They also tell us a great deal about Turks. I'll never be able to visit Turkey again without noticing its sitters. With one quick insight Pritchett has caught a whole national trait. This is the essence of good writing about a place. Distill the important from the immaterial.

I'm reminded by Pritchett's own nationality that the English have long excelled at a distinctive form of travel writing that I should mention before traveling on—the article that is less notable for what the writer extracts from a place than for what the place extracts from him. New sights touch off thoughts that would otherwise never have entered his mind. If travel is broadening, it should broaden more than just our knowledge of, say, how a Gothic cathedral looks or how the French make wine. It should generate a whole constellation of new ideas about how men and women work and play, raise their children, worship their gods, live and die. Certainly the books written by Britain's "desert eccentrics"—scholar-adventurers like Charles Doughty and T. E. Lawrence, who chose to live among the Arabs—derive much of their strange power from the reflections born of surviving in so harsh and minimal an environment.

So when you write about a place, try to draw the best out of it. But if the process should work in reverse, let it draw the best out of you. In this sense, probably the finest travel book written by an American is *Walden*, though Thoreau only went a few miles out of town, and today a growing number of nonfiction writers are finding their voice by hitting the road, going back to the land or pondering the mysteries of nature.

No writer has been more creatively provoked by the search for modern America than Norman Mailer. Shrewd and witty insights about our latest values fly like sparks out of his books—typically, his book about the launching of Apollo 11, *Of a Fire on the Moon*, and about the faceless new breed of men who reared it and raised it into space. What did it all mean? Was the achievement stirring or sterile? Even Mailer isn't sure at the end, and Mailer is seldom at a loss for certitudes. But there has been much to think about along the way.

Let me leave you with him, then, on the eve of the launch, staring with "some portion of a million" rubber-neckers across the water to the spaceship that would lift itself off its pad in the morning and take three men to the moon:

> In the distance she glowed for all the world like some white stone Madonna in the mountains, welcoming foot-sore travelers at dusk. Perhaps it was an unforeseen game of the lighting, but America had not had its movie premieres for nothing, nor its Rockettes in Radio City and 50 million squares tooling the tourist miles over the years to Big Town to buy a ticket to spectacle and back home again. If you were going to have a Hollywood premiere and arc lights, a million out to watch and a space-ship which looked across the evening flutter like the light on the Shrine of Our Lady outside any church in Brooklyn or Bay Ridge, then by God you might just as well have this spectacle on the premiere trip to the moon. That deserved a searchlight or two!
>
> There were new industries in America these years. After five decades of suspense movies, and movies of the Wild West, after the adventures of several generations of men in two world wars and Korea and Vietnam, after 16 years of *Playboy* and American iconization of

the gravity-defying breast and the sun-ripened buttock, after ten years of the greatest professional football, after a hundred years and more of a tradition that the frontier was open and would never close, and after 20 more perplexing technological years when prosperity came to nearly every White pocket, and technology put out its plastic, its superhighways, its supermarkets, its appliances, its suburbs, its smog, and its intimation that the frontier was damn shut, shut like a boulder on a rabbit burrow, America had erupted from this pressure between its love of adventure and its fear that adventure was completely shut down; America had spewed out on the road. The country had become a nation of campers, of cars toting trailers, of cars pulling tent-trailers, of truck-campers, top-of-car tent packs, Volkswagen buses converted to ambulatory bedrooms, jeeps with Chic Sale houses built on the back, Land-Rovers with bunks, Broncos with more bunks—any way a man could get out of the house with his buddies or his family or his grandmother, and take to the road and find some ten by twenty feet of grass not posted, not tenanted, and not too muddy, he would camp. All over America in the summer the night fields were now filled with Americans sleeping on air mattresses which reposed on plastic cloth floors of plastic cloth tents—what a sweet smell of Corporate Chemical, what a vat and void to mix with all the balmy fermy chlorophylls and pollens of nature! America the Sanitary, and America the Wild, went out to sleep in the woods, Sanitary-Lobe and Wild-Lobe nesting neatly together, schizophrenic twins in the skull case of the good family American.

14. Bits & Pieces

This is a chapter of scraps and morsels—small admonitions on many points that I have collected under one, as they say, umbrella.

VERBS. Use active verbs unless there is no comfortable way to get around using a passive verb. The difference between an active-verb style and a passive-verb style—in pace, clarity and vigor—is the difference between life and death for a writer.

"Joe hit him" is strong. "He was hit by Joe" is weak. The first is short and vivid and direct; it leaves no doubt about who did what. The second is necessarily longer and it has an insipid quality; something was done by somebody to someone else. A style that consists mainly of passive constructions, especially if the sentences are long, saps the reader's energy. He is never quite certain of what is being perpetrated by whom and on whom.

I use "perpetrated" because it's the kind of word that passive-tense writers are fond of. They prefer long words of Latin origin to short Anglo-Saxon words—which compounds their trouble and makes their sentences still more glutinous. Short is generally better than long. (Of the 701 words in Lincoln's Second Inaugural Address, a marvel of economy in itself, 505 are words of one syllable and 122 are words of two syllables.)

Verbs are the most important of all your tools. They push the sentence forward and give it momentum. Active verbs push hard; passive verbs tug fitfully. Most verbs also carry somewhere in their imagery or in their sound a suggestion of what they mean: flail, poke, dazzle, squash, beguile, pamper, swagger, wheedle, vex. Probably no other language has such a vast supply of verbs so bright with color. Don't choose one that is dull or merely serviceable. Make active verbs activate your sentences, and try to avoid the kind that need an appended preposition or two to complete their work. Don't set up a business that you can start or launch. Don't face up to a problem that you can confront.

Cultivate this rich crop. And if you want to see how active verbs give vitality and flair to the written word, don't just go back to Hemingway or Thurber or Thoreau. I commend the King James Bible and William Shakespeare.

ADVERBS. Most adverbs are unnecessary. You will clutter your sentence and annoy the reader if you choose a verb that has a precise meaning and then add an adverb that carries the same meaning. Don't tell us that the radio blared loudly—"blare" connotes loudness. Don't write that someone clenched his teeth tightly—there is no other way to clench teeth. Again and again in careless writing, self-sufficient verbs are weakened by redundant adverbs.

So are countless adjectives and other parts of speech: "Totally flabbergasted," "effortlessly easy," "slightly spartan." The beauty of "flabbergasted" is that it implies an astonishment that is total; I can't picture anyone being partly flabbergasted. If an action is so easy as to be effortless, use "effortless." And what is "slightly spartan"? Perhaps a monk's cell with wall-to-wall carpeting.

Don't use adverbs unless they do some work. If an athlete loses a game because he played badly, "badly" gives us the helpful information that he didn't play well. But spare us the news that he moped dejectedly and that the winner grinned widely.

ADJECTIVES. Most adjectives are also unnecessary. Like adverbs, they are sprinkled into sentences by writers who don't stop to think that the concept is already in the noun. This kind of prose is littered with precipitous cliffs and lacy spiderwebs and doleful mourners and friendly smiles. It is also littered with adjectives denoting the color of an object whose color is well known: yellow daffodils and brownish dirt. If you want to make a value judgment about daffodils, choose an adjective like "garish." If you're in a section of the country where the dirt is red, feel free to mention the red dirt. These adjectives would do a job that the noun wouldn't be doing.

Redundant adjectives are only part of the problem. Most writers sow adjectives almost unconsciously into the soil of their prose to make it more lush and pretty. The sentences become longer and longer as they fill up with stately elms and frisky kittens and hard-bitten detectives and sleepy lagoons. This is adjective-by-habit, and it's a habit you should stop. Not every oak has to be gnarled. The adjective that exists solely as decoration is a self-indulgence for the writer and an obstacle for the reader.

Again, the rule is simple: Make your adjectives do work that needs to be done. "He looked at the gray sky and the black clouds and decided to sail back to the harbor." The darkness of the sky is the reason for the decision. If it's important to tell the reader that a house was drab or that a girl was beautiful, by all means use "drab" and "beautiful." They will have their proper power because you have learned to use adjectives sparsely.

LITTLE QUALIFIERS. Prune out the small words that qualify how you feel and how you think and what you saw: "a bit," "a little," "sort of," "kind of," "rather," "quite," "very," "too," "pretty much," "in a very real sense" and dozens more. They dilute both your style and your persuasiveness.

Don't say you were a bit confused and sort of tired and a little depressed and somewhat annoyed. Be tired. Be confused. Be depressed. Be annoyed. Don't hedge your prose with little timidities. Good writing is lean and confident.

Don't say you weren't too happy because the hotel looked pretty expensive. Say you weren't happy because the hotel looked expensive. Don't tell us that you were quite fortunate. How fortunate is that?

Don't describe an event as rather spectacular or very awesome. Words like "spectacular" and "awesome" don't submit to measurement. "Very" is a useful word to achieve emphasis, but far more often it is clutter. There's no need to call someone very methodical. Either he is methodical or he isn't.

The larger point here is one of authority. Every little qualifier whittles away some fraction of trust on the part of the reader. He wants a writer who believes in himself and in what he is saying. Don't diminish this belief. Don't be kind of bold. Be bold.

PUNCTUATION. These are brief thoughts on punctuation, in no way intended as a primer. If you don't know how to punctuate—and many college students still don't—get a grammar book.

The Period. There's not much to be said about the period except that most writers don't reach it soon enough. If you find yourself hopelessly mired in a long sentence, it's probably because you're trying to make the sentence do more than it can reasonably do—perhaps express two dissimilar thoughts. The quickest way out is to break the long sentence into two short sentences, or even three. There is no minimum length for a sentence that's acceptable in the eyes of man and God. Among good writers it is the short sentence that predominates, and don't tell me about Norman Mailer—he's a genius. If you want to write long sentences, be a genius. Or at least make sure that the sentence is under control from beginning to end, in syntax and punctuation, so that the reader knows where he is at every step of the winding trail.

The Exclamation Point. Don't use it unless you must to achieve a certain effect. It has a gushy aura—the breathless excitement of a debutante commenting on an event that was exciting only to her: "Daddy says I must have had too much champagne!" "But honestly, I just could have danced all night!" We have all suffered more than our share of these sentences in which an exclamation point knocks us over the head with how cute or wonderful something was. Instead, construct your sentence so that the order of the words will put the emphasis where you want it. Also resist using the exclamation point to notify the reader that you are making a joke or being ironic. "It never occurred to me that the water pistol might be loaded!" The reader is annoyed by your reminder that this was a comical moment. He is also robbed of the pleasure of making the discovery himself. Humor is best achieved by understatement, and there's nothing subtle about an exclamation point.

The Semicolon. There is a nineteenth-century mustiness that hangs over the semicolon. We associate it with the carefully balanced sentences, the judicious weighing of "on the one hand" and "on the other hand," of Conrad and Thackeray and Hardy. Therefore it should be used sparingly by writers of nonfiction today. Yet I notice that it turns up often in the excerpts I've quoted in this book, and I've used it here myself more than I ordinarily do, mainly for the classic purpose of weighing two sides of the same problem. Still, the semicolon does bring the reader, if not to a halt, at least to a considerable pause. So use it with discretion, remembering that it will slow to a Victorian pace the twentieth-century momentum you are striving for, and rely instead on the period and the dash.

The Dash. Somehow this invaluable tool is widely regarded as not quite proper—a bumpkin at the genteel dinner table of good English. But it has full membership and will get you out of many tight corners. The dash is used in two different ways. One is to amplify or justify in the second part of the sentence a thought you have stated in the first part. "We decided to keep going—it was only 100 miles more and we could get there in time for dinner." By its very shape the dash pushes the sentence ahead and explains why they decided to keep going. The other use involves two dashes, which set apart a parenthetical thought within a longer sentence. "She told me to get in the car—she had been after me all summer to have a haircut—and we drove silently into town." An explanatory detail that might otherwise have had to go into a separate sentence is dispatched along the way.

The Colon. The colon has begun to look even more antique than the semicolon, and many of its functions have been taken over by the dash. But it still serves well its pure role of bringing your sentence to a brief halt before you plunge into, say, a quotation or an itemized list. "The brochure said that the ship would stop at the following ports: Oran, Algiers, Naples, Brindisi, Piraeus, Istanbul and Beirut." You can't beat the colon for work like that.

MOOD CHANGERS. Learn to alert the reader as early as possible in a sentence to any change in mood from the previous sentence. At least a dozen words will do this job for you: "but," "yet," "however," "nevertheless," "still," "instead," "thus," "therefore," "meanwhile," "now," "later," "today," "subsequently" and several more. I can't overstate how much easier it is for the reader to process a sentence if you start with "but" when you're shifting direction, or, conversely, how much harder it is if he must wait until the end to realize that you're now in a different gear.

Many of us were taught that no sentence should begin with "but." If that's what you learned, unlearn it—there is no stronger word at the start. It announces total contrast with what has gone before, and the reader is primed for the change. If you need relief from too many sentences beginning with "but," switch to "however." It is, however, a weaker word and therefore needs careful placement. Don't start a sentence with "however"—it hangs there like a wet dishrag. And don't end with "however"—by that time it has lost its "howeverness." Put it as early as you reasonably can—as I did three sentences ago. Its abruptness then becomes a virtue.

"Yet" does almost the same job as "but," though its meaning is closer to "nevertheless." Either of these words at the beginning of a sentence—"Yet he decided to go" or "Nevertheless he decided to go"—can replace a whole long phrase that summarizes what the reader has just been told: "Despite the fact that all these dangers had been pointed out to him, he decided to go." Look for all the places where one of these short words will quickly convey the same mood and meaning as a long and dismal clause. "Instead I took the train." "Still I had to admire him." "Thus I learned how to smoke." "It was therefore easy to meet him." "Meanwhile I had talked to John." What a vast amount of huffing and puffing these pivotal words save! (The exclamation point is to show that I really mean it.)

As for "meanwhile," "now," "today" and "later," what they also save is confusion, for writers often change their time context without remembering to tip the reader off. "Now I know better." "Today you can't find such an item." "Later I found out why." Always make sure that the reader is oriented. Keep asking yourself where you left him in the previous sentence.

CONTRACTIONS. Your style will obviously be warmer and truer to your personality if you use contractions like "I'll" and "won't" when they fit comfortably into what you're writing. "I'll be glad to see them if they don't get mad" is less stiff than "I will be glad to see them if they do not get mad." There's no rule against such informality—trust your ear and your instincts. I only suggest avoiding one form—"I'd," "he'd," "we'd," etc.—because "I'd" can mean both "I had" and "I would," and the reader must often get well into a sentence before learning which meaning it is. Frequently it turns out to be not the one he thought it was. Also, don't invent contractions, like "could've." Stick with the ones you can find in the dictionary.

OVERSTATEMENT. "The living room looked as if an atomic bomb had gone off there," writes the inexperienced writer, describing what he saw on Sunday morning after a Saturday night party that got out of hand. Well, we all know that he's exaggerating to make a droll point, but we also know that an atomic bomb *didn't* go off there, or any other bomb except maybe a water bomb. "I felt as if ten 747 jets were flying through my brain," he says, "and I seriously considered jumping out the window and killing myself." These verbal high jinks can get just so high—and I'm already well over the limit—before the reader feels an overpowering drowsiness. It's like being trapped with a man who can't stop reciting limericks. Don't overstate. You didn't really consider jumping out the window. Life has more than enough truly horrible funny situations. Let the humor sneak up so that we hardly hear it coming.

CREDIBILITY. Credibility is just as fragile for a writer as for a President. Don't inflate an incident to make it more flamboyant or bizarre than it actually was. If the reader catches you in just one bogus statement that you are trying to pass off as true, everything that you write thereafter will be suspect. It's too great a risk, and not worth taking.

CONCEPT NOUNS. Nouns that express a concept are commonly used in bad writing instead of verbs that tell what somebody did. Here are three typical dead sentences:

"The common reaction is incredulous laughter."

"Bemused cynicism isn't the only response to the old system."

"The current campus hostility is a symptom of the change."

What is so eerie about these sentences is that they have no people in them. They also have no working verbs—only "is" or "isn't." The reader can't visualize anybody performing some task; the meaning all lies in impersonal nouns that embody a vague concept: "reaction," "cynicism," "response," "hostility." Turn these cold sentences around. Get people doing things:

"Most people just laugh with disbelief."

"Some people respond to the old system by turning cynical; others say . . ."

"It's easy to notice the change—you can see how angry all the students are."

My revised sentences aren't jumping with vigor, partly because the material I'm trying to knead into shape is shapeless dough. But at least they have real people and real verbs. Don't get caught holding a bag that doesn't have anything in it but abstract nouns. You'll sink to the bottom of the lake and never be seen again.

CREEPING NOUNISM. This is a new American disease that strings two or three nouns together where one will do. Nobody goes broke now; we have money problem areas. It no longer rains; we have precipitation activity. Choose one noun, preferably one that's short and specific. Choose it carefully and it will do the job.

SEXISM. Probably the most vexing new question for writers is what to do about the "he-she" pronoun. The feminist movement has demonstrated how much sexism lurks in our language, not only in the bothersome "he," but in the hundreds of words that carry an invidious meaning or some overtone of judgment. They are words which patronize ("gal"), or which imply second-class status ("poetess") or a second-class role ("housewife") or a certain kind of empty-headedness ("the girls"), or which demean the ability of a woman to do a man's job ("lady lawyer"), or which are deliberately prurient ("divorcée," "coed," "blonde") and which are seldom applied to men. Men get mugged; a woman who gets mugged is a shapely stewardess or a pert brunette.

Just as damaging—and more subtle—are the countless usages that treat women as possessions of the family male, not as people with their own identity who played an equal part in the family saga: "Early settlers pushed west with their wives and children." Turn those settlers into pioneer families, or pioneer couples who went west with their sons and daughters, or men and women who settled the West. Today there are very few roles or jobs that aren't open to both sexes. Don't ever use constructions which suggest that only men can be settlers or farmers or firefighters. Good writers and editors are now pushing these stereotypes out of the language.

A thornier problem is raised by the feminists' annoyance with words that contain "man," such as "chairman" and "spokesman." Their point, of course, is that women can chair a committee as well as a man and that they are equally good at spoking. Hence the flurry of new words like "chairperson" and "spokeswoman." These makeshift words served a larger purpose throughout the 1970s of raising our consciousness about sex discrimination both in words and in attitudes. But in the end they are makeshift words, perhaps hurting the cause more than helping it. My own feeling is that they will now begin to fade. "Chairman" is an honorable title, and I prefer it to "chairperson" or "chairwoman." So, I think, will most of the women in the 1980s who become chairman of a company or a board. The main battle—to prove that women can assume traditionally male jobs—is rapidly being won.

This still leaves the problem of the pronoun. Obviously "he" and "him" and "his" are words that rankle. "Every employee should decide what he thinks is best for him and his dependents." What are we to do about these countless sentences? One solution is to turn them into the plural: "All employees should decide what they think is best for them and their dependents." But this cure is good only in small doses. Plurals are weaker than singulars. The singular is particular and concrete, and a style that converts every "he" into a "they" will quickly turn to mush.

Another common solution is to use "or": "Every employee should decide what he or she thinks is best for him or her." But, again, it can only be used sparingly. Often a writer will find several situations in an article where he or she can use "he or she," or "him or her," if it seems natural. By "natural" I mean that the writer is serving notice that he (or she) has the problem in mind and is trying his (or her) best within reasonable limits. But let's face it: the English language is stuck with the generic masculine ("Man shall not live by bread alone"). To turn every "he" into a "he or she," and every "his" into a "his or her," would thicken the language and make it much harder to read. This book, for instance, would be longer and drearier if I used "he or she" with every mention of "the writer" and "the reader." I reject "he/she" altogether; the slant has no place in good English.

The best solutions simply eliminate male pronouns and connotations by altering some component of the sentence. "We" is a useful substitute for "he"; "the" can often replace "his"; general nouns can replace specific nouns: (A) "First he notices what's happening to his kids and he blames it on his neighborhood." (B) "First we notice what's happening to our kids and we blame it on the neighborhood." (A) "Doctors often neglect their wives and children." (B) "Doctors often neglect their families." Countless sins can be erased by such small changes.

The pedants, of course, have other solutions. They have proposed various unisex pronouns, deriving from Nordic or Anglo-Saxon roots that only they have dug up, which they claim would fall easily into our speech if we just started teaching them in our schools and writing them in our writings. One of their typical candidates is "thon," a third-person pronoun that applies to either gender and has a handy possessive ("thons") and reflexive ("thonself"). Maybe I don't speak for the average American, but I very much doubt that thon wants that word in thons language or that thon would use it thonself. This is not how language changes.

PARAGRAPHS. Keep your paragraphs short, especially if you're writing for a newspaper or a magazine that sets its type in a narrow width. This is purely visual and psychological advice.

Short paragraphs put air around what you write and make it look inviting, whereas one long chunk of type can discourage the reader from even starting to read. A newspaper paragraph generally shouldn't have more than two or three sentences. You may worry that such frequent paragraphing will damage the logical development of your idea. (Obviously *The New Yorker* is obsessed by this fear—a reader can go for several columns without relief.) Don't worry. The gains far outweigh the dangers.

DICTATION. Much of the "writing" done in America is done by dictation. Administrators, executives, managers, bureaucrats and other officials think in terms of using their time efficiently. To them the quickest way of getting something "written" is to dictate it to a secretary and never look at it. This is false economy—they save a few hours and blow their whole personality. Dictated sentences tend to be pompous, sloppy and redundant. If an executive is so busy that he can't avoid dictating, he should at least find time to edit what he has dictated, crossing words out and putting words in, making sure that what he finally writes is a true reflection of who he is, especially if it's a document that will go to a large number of readers who will judge him as a person on the basis of his style.

WRITING IS NOT A CONTEST. Every writer is starting from a different point and is bound for a different destination. Yet many writers are paralyzed by the thought that they are competing with everybody else who is trying to write and is presumably doing it better. This can often happen, for instance, in a writing class. Inexperienced students are chilled to find themselves in the same class with students whose byline has appeared in the college newspaper. But writing for the college paper is no great credential; in fact, I've often found that the hares who write for the paper are overtaken by the tortoises who move resolutely toward the goal of mastering the craft. The same fear cripples the lonely free-lance writer, who sees the work of other writers appearing in magazines while his own keeps returning in the mail. Forget the competition and go at your own pace. Ultimately your only contest is with yourself.

THE SUBCONSCIOUS MIND. Your subconscious mind does more writing than you think. Often you'll spend a whole day trying to fight your way out of some verbal thicket in which you seem to be tangled beyond salvation. Surprisingly often a solution will occur to you the next morning when you plunge back in. While you slept, your writer's mind didn't. To some extent a writer is always working. Stay alert to the currents around you. Much of what you see and hear will come back, having percolated for days or even months through your subconscious mind, just when your conscious mind, laboring over the typewriter, needs it.

THE QUICKEST FIX. Surprisingly often a difficult problem in a sentence can be solved by simply getting rid of it. Unfortunately, this solution is usually the last one that occurs to the writer trying to disentangle himself. First he will put the troublesome phrase through all kinds of exertions—moving it to some other part of the sentence, trying to rephrase it, adding new words to clarify the thought or to oil whatever is stuck. These laborious efforts only make the situation worse, and the writer is left to conclude that there *is* no solution to his problem—not a comforting thought. When you find yourself at such an impasse, look at the troublesome element and ask, "Do I need it at all?" Probably you don't. It was trying to do an unnecessary job all along—that's why it was giving you so much grief. Remove it and watch the afflicted sentence spring to life and breathe normally. It's the quickest possible cure and, very often, the best.

BREEZINESS. There is a style of writing that's so seemingly relaxed that you think you hear the author talking to you. E. B. White is probably its best practitioner, though many other masters of the form—James Thurber, Lewis Thomas, Virgil Thomson—come to mind. I'm partial to it because it's the style that I've always tried to write myself. The common assumption about the style is that it is effortless. Just the opposite is true: the effortless style is achieved by strenuous effort and rewriting. The nails of grammar and syntax are all in place; the English is as good as the writer can make it, and the total piece has a design that pulls the reader along from start to finish.

Here, for instance, is how a typical piece by E. B. White begins:

> I spent several days and nights in mid-September with an ailing pig and I feel driven to account for this stretch of time, more particularly since the pig died at last, and I lived, and things might easily have gone the other way round and none left to do the accounting.

At first glance the sentence is so folksy that we imagine ourselves sitting in the parlor of White's house in rural Maine. A wood fire is burning and White is in a rocking chair, puffing on a pipe. He wants to tell us a yarn, and the words just tumble out. But look at the sentence again. It's a thing of beauty; nothing about it is accidental. Its use of the English language is disciplined. The punctuation is formal, the words are plain and precise, and the rhythm is that of a poet, a man who writes by ear.

This is the effortless style at its best: a methodical act of writing that disarms us with its generated warmth. The writer knows exactly what he's doing; he's writing with confidence, and—most important—he's writing to please himself. He's not trying to ingratiate himself with the reader. He knows that if he pleases himself a certain number of readers will also enjoy what he has to say.

Inexperienced writers miss this point. They think that all they have to do to achieve a casual effect is to be "just folks"—good old Bob or Betty chatting over the back fence. They're so eager not to appear highbrow that they don't even try to write good English. They want to be a pal to the reader and to make his reading simple. What they write is the breezy style.

How would a breezy writer handle E. B. White's vigil with the pig? It might come out like this:

> Ever stay up late babysitting for a sick porker? Believe me, you can lose a heckuva lot of shuteye. I did this bit for three nights back in September and my better half thought I'd lost my marbles. (Just kidding, Pam!) Frankly, the whole deal kind of bummed me out. Because, you see, the pig up and died on me. To tell you the truth, I wasn't feeling in the pink myself, so I suppose it could have been yours truly and not old Porky who kicked the bucket. And you can bet your bottom dollar Mr. Pig wasn't going to write any book about it.

I won't labor all the obvious reasons why this stuff is so terrible. It's crude. It's corny. It's verbose. It's disdainful of the English language. It's condescending. But the most pathetic thing about the breezy style is that it's harder to read than good English. In the writer's desperate attempt to simplify the reader's journey he has strewn the path with obstacles: cheap slang, shoddy sentences, windy musings. E. B. White's style is infinitely easier to read. He knows that the tools of grammar haven't survived for so many centuries by chance—they are roadmarks that the reader not only needs but subconsciously wants. Nobody ever stopped reading E. B. White or V. S. Pritchett because the writing was too good. But a reader will stop if he thinks the writer is talking down to him. Nobody wants to be patronized.

Write with respect for the English language at its best and for the reader at his best.

TASTE. What finally separates the good writer from the breezy writer is a quality so intangible that nobody even knows what it is: taste. It can't be defined, but we know it when we see it. A woman with taste in clothes delights us with her ability to turn herself out every day in a combination that's not only stylish and surprising; it's also exactly right. Taste is the instinct to know what works and to avoid what doesn't.

In the arts, knowing what not to do is a major component of taste. Two jazz pianists may be equally proficient at the keyboard. The one with taste will put every note to useful work in telling his story; the one without taste will drench us in ripples and other unnecessary ornaments. A painter with taste will trust his eye to tell him what needs to be on his canvas and what doesn't; the one without taste will give us a landscape that's too pretty, or too cluttered, or too gaudy in its colors—anyway, too something.

I realize that I'm trying to pin down a matter that's highly subjective and that has no firm rules. One man's beautiful painting is another man's kitsch. It's also true that taste changes with the decades—yesterday's charm is rejected today as junk, but tomorrow it will be back in vogue, certified once again as charming. So why do I even bring the problem up? Mainly to remind you that it exists. Taste is an invisible current that runs through all writing, and you should be aware of it.

Sometimes, in fact, it's not invisible. Every art form has a hard core of verities that survive the fickleness of time. There must be something innately pleasing, for instance, in the proportions of the Parthenon; Western man continues to let the Greeks of two thousand years ago design his major public buildings. In music, the fugues of Bach have a timeless elegance that's rooted in the timeless laws of mathematics.

Does writing have any such guideposts for us? Not many—writing is the expression of every person's individuality, and in general we can only say that we know what we like when it comes along. Still, as in the other arts, taste is partly a question of knowing what to omit. Clichés, for example. If a writer litters his prose with platitudes—if every idea is first and foremost and in the last analysis one that hits the nail on the head—we can safely infer that the writer lacks an instinct for what gives language its freshness. Faced with a choice between the novel and the banal, he goes unerringly for the banal.

Extend the point beyond clichés to include a writer's larger use of words. Again, freshness is a critical factor. Taste chooses words that have originality, strength and precision; non-taste veers into the breezy vernacular of the alumni magazine's class notes—a world where people in authority are the top brass or the powers-that-be. What exactly is wrong with "the top brass"? Nothing—and everything. Taste is knowing that it's better to call people in authority what they are: officials, or executives, or the president of the company. Non-taste reaches for the cute synonym.

But finally taste is a mixture of qualities that are beyond defining: an ear, for instance, that can hear the difference between a sentence that limps and a sentence that lilts, or an intuition that knows when a casual phrase dropped into a formal sentence will not only feel right but will seem to be the inevitable choice. Does this mean that taste can't be learned? Yes and no. Perfect taste, like perfect pitch, is a gift from God. But a certain amount can be acquired. The trick is to study those who have it.

IMITATION. Don't ever hesitate to imitate another writer—every artist learning his craft needs some models. Eventually you'll find your own voice and shed the skin of the writer you imitated. But pick only the best models. If you want to write about medicine, read Lewis Thomas; if you want to write literary criticism, read Edmund Wilson and Alfred Kazin.

The best way to learn to write is to study the work of the men and women who are doing the kind of writing you want to do. I learned to write mainly by reading other writers. In fact, I still read E. B. White occasionally to get myself warmed up. I want to get his cadences into my ear—and also his taste, by which I mean his attitude toward language. I still read some S. J. Perelman before starting a piece of humor. I want to get into my head his relish of nonsense and his pleasure in pushing the language to its outer limits. Find the models that are right for you and make them your mentors.

ELOQUENCE AND THE USES OF THE PAST. By reading other writers you plug yourself into a longer tradition that enriches you. Sometimes, in fact, you will tap a vein of eloquence or racial memory that gives your writing a depth it could never attain on its own. Let me illustrate what I mean by a roundabout route.

Normally I don't read the proclamations issued by state officials to designate important days of the year as important days of the year. But in 1976, when I was at Yale, the governor of Connecticut, Ella Grasso, had the pleasant idea of reissuing the Thanksgiving Proclamation written forty years earlier by Governor Wilbur Cross, which she called "a masterpiece of eloquence." I've often wondered whether eloquence has vanished from American life and speech, or whether we even still consider it a goal worth striving for. So I studied Governor Cross's words to see how they had weathered the passage of time, that cruel judge of the rhetoric of earlier generations. I was delighted to find that I agreed with Mrs. Grasso. It was a piece written by a master:

> Time out of mind at this turn of the seasons when the
> hardy oak leaves rustle in the wind and the frost gives a
> tang to the air and the dusk falls early and the friendly

evenings lengthen under the heel of Orion, it has seemed good to our people to join together in praising the Creator and Preserver, who has brought us by a way that we did not know to the end of another year. In observance of this custom, I appoint Thursday, the 26th of November, as a day of Public Thanksgiving for the blessings that have been our common lot and have placed our beloved state with the favored regions of earth—for all the creature comforts: the yield of the soil that has fed us and the richer yield from labor of every kind that has sustained our lives—and for all those things, as dear as breath to the body, that quicken man's faith in his manhood, that nourish and strengthen his word and act; for honor held above price; for steadfast courage and zeal in the long, long search after truth; for liberty and for justice freely granted by each to his fellow and so as freely enjoyed; and for the crowning glory and mercy of peace upon our land;—that we may humbly take heart of these blessings as we gather once again with solemn and festive rites to our Harvest Home.

Mrs. Grasso added a postscript urging the citizens of Connecticut "to renew their dedication to the spirit of sacrifice and commitment which the Pilgrims invoked during their first harsh winter in the New World," and I made a mental note to look at Orion that night. I was glad to be reminded that I was living in one of the favored regions of earth. I was also glad to be reminded that peace is not the only crowning glory to be thankful for; so is the English language when it is gracefully used for the public good. The cadences of Jefferson, Lincoln, Churchill, Roosevelt and Adlai Stevenson came rolling down to me. (The cadences of Truman, Eisenhower and Nixon did not.)

I posted the Thanksgiving proclamation on a bulletin

board for my students to enjoy. From their comments I realized that several of them thought I was being facetious.
Knowing my obsession with simplicity, they assumed that I
regarded Governor Cross's message as florid excess.

The incident left me with several questions. Had I sprung
Wilbur Cross's prose on a generation that had never been
exposed to nobility of language as a means of addressing the
populace? I couldn't recall a single attempt since John F.
Kennedy's inaugural speech in 1961. This was a generation
reared on television, where the picture is valued more
highly than the word—where the word, in fact, is devalued,
used as mere punctuation or chatter, and often misused and
mispronounced. It was also a generation reared on music—
songs and rhythms meant to be heard and felt. With so
much noise in the air from TV sets and stereo sets, was any
American child being trained to listen? Was anyone calling
attention to the majesty of a well-constructed sentence?

My other question raised a more subtle mystery: What is
the line that separates eloquence from bombast? Why are we
exalted by the words of Wilbur Cross and anesthetized by
the speeches of most politicians and public officials who ply
us with oratorical ruffles and flourishes?

Part of the answer takes us back to taste. A writer with an
ear for language will reach for fresh imagery and avoid
phrases that are trite. The hack will reach for the very
clichés that the good writer spurns, thinking that he will en-
rich his thoughts with currency that is, as he would put it,
tried and true. Another part of the answer lies in simplicity.
Writing that will endure tends to consist of words that are
short and strong; words that anesthetize are words of three,
four and five syllables, mostly of Latin origin, many of them
ending in "ion" and embodying a vague concept. In Wilbur
Cross's Thanksgiving Proclamation there are no four-syllable
words and only ten three-syllable words, three of which are
proper nouns that he was stuck with. Also notice how many

of the governor's words are anything but vague: leaves, wind, frost, air, evening, earth, comforts, soil, labor, breath, body, justice, courage, peace, land, rites, home. They are homely words in the best sense. They catch the rhythm of the seasons and the dailiness of life.

But ultimately eloquence runs on a deeper current. It moves us with what it leaves unsaid, touching off echoes in what we already know from our reading, our religion and our heritage. Eloquence invites us to bring some part of ourselves to the transaction. It was no accident that Lincoln's speeches resounded with echoes of the King James Bible. He knew it almost by heart from his boyhood, and he had so soaked himself in its sonorities that his formal English was more Elizabethan than American. The Second Inaugural Address reverberates with Biblical phrases and paraphrases: "It may seem strange that any men should dare to ask a just God's assistance in wringing their bread from the sweat of other men's faces, but let us judge not, that we be not judged." The first half of the sentence borrows a metaphor from Genesis, the second half reshapes a famous command in Matthew, and "a just God" is from Isaiah.

If this speech affects me more than any other American document, it's not only because I know that Lincoln was killed five weeks later, or because I'm moved by all the pain that culminated in this plea for a reconciliation that would have malice toward none and charity for all. It's also because Lincoln tapped some of Western man's oldest teachings about slavery, clemency and judgment. His words carried stern overtones for the men and women who heard him in 1865, reared, as he was, on the Bible. But even in the 1980s it's hard not to feel a wrath almost too ancient to grasp in Lincoln's notion that God might will the Civil War to continue "until all the wealth piled by the bondsman's two hundred and fifty years of unrequited toil shall be sunk, and until every drop of blood drawn with the lash shall be paid by another drawn with the sword, as was said three thousand years ago."

Wilbur Cross's Thanksgiving Proclamation also echoes with truths that we know in our bones. To such mysteries as the changing of the seasons and the bounty of the earth we bring strong emotions of our own. Who hasn't looked with awe at Orion? To such democratic processes as "the long search after truth" and "liberty and justice freely granted" we bring fragments of our own searches after truth, our own grantings and receivings, in a nation where so many human rights have been won and so many still elude us. Governor Cross doesn't take our time to explain these processes, and I'm grateful to him for that. I hate to think how many clichés a hack orator would marshal to tell us far more—and nourish us far less.

Therefore remember the uses of the past when you tell your story. What moves us in writing that has regional or ethnic roots—black writing, Southern writing, Jewish-American writing—is the sound of voices far older than the narrator's, talking in languages that are more than ordinarily rich. Toni Morrison, one of the most eloquent of black writers, once said: "I remember the language of the people I grew up with. Language was so important to them. All that power was in it. And grace and metaphor. Some of it was very formal and Biblical, because the habit is that when you have something important to say you go into parable, if you're from Africa, or you go into another level of language. I wanted to use language that way. Because my feeling was that a black novel was not black because I wrote it, or because there were black people in it, or because it was about black things. It was the style. It had a certain style. It was inevitable. I couldn't describe it, but I could produce it."

Go with what seems inevitable in your own heritage. Embrace it naturally and it may lead you to eloquence.

15. Science Writing and Technical Writing

Take a class of writing students in a liberal arts college, tell them that their next assignment is to write on some aspect of science, and a pitiful moan will go around the room. "No! Not science!" the moan says. "Don't make us enter that dread region whose mysteries can only be fathomed by other scientists."

My sympathy is with them. I'm not much farther along myself than James Thurber's grandmother, who thought that "electricity was dripping invisibly all over the house" from wall sockets. But as a writer I know that a complex subject can be made as accessible to the layman as a simple subject. It's just a question of putting one sentence after another. The "after," however, is unusually important. Nowhere else must you work so hard to write sentences that form a linear sequence. This is no place for fanciful leaps or implied truths. Fact and deduction are the ruling family.

The assignment I gave to students was a seemingly primitive one. I just asked them to describe how something works. I didn't care about a seductive lead or a surprise ending or any connecting devices. I only wanted them to tell me, say, how a sewing machine does what it does, or a bicycle, or why an apple falls down, or how the eye tells the brain what it sees. Any process will do, and science can be defined loosely to include technology, medicine and nature.

It's a tenet of journalism that "the reader knows nothing."

133

As tenets go, it's not too complimentary, but the writer will forget it at his peril. You just can't assume that people know what you think any boob knows, or that they still remember what has once been explained to them. I doubt, for instance, if I could get into one of those life jackets that hundreds of airline stewardesses have demonstrated to me: something about pulling two toggle knobs sharply downward (or is it sideways?). And just where are those straps that I "simply" have to slip into, the snaps that I "simply" have to snap?

Describing how a process works is valuable for two reasons. First it forces you to make sure that *you* know how it works. Then it forces you to make sure that the reader will understand it as clearly as you do. In fact, I found it to be a breakthrough assignment for many students who couldn't disentangle themselves from vagueness, clutter and disorderly thinking.

One of them, a sophomore still immobilized in these swamps at mid-term—a bright mind spraying the page with fuzzy thoughts—was in a joyful mood when he brought me his piece on how a fire extinguisher works. I was dubious. But the piece was lucid. It explained how different kinds of fires are specifically attacked by different kinds of extinguishers. It moved with absolute simplicity and logic. I was elated by his overnight change into a writer who had learned the secret of writing sequentially. By the end of his junior year he had written and published a "how to" book that sold better than any book *I* had written, and he has since published several more.

Many other students who were equally adrift went through the same miracle cure and have written with clarity ever since. For the principle of science writing applies to *all* nonfiction writing. It's the principle of leading a reader who knows nothing, step by step, to a grasp of the subject. Once you learn it, remember it in every article you write.

Let me tilt the linear example by 90 degrees and ask you

to imagine science writing as an upside-down pyramid. Start at the bottom with the one fact that a reader must know before he can learn any more. The second sentence broadens what was stated first, making the pyramid wider, and the third sentence broadens the second, so that gradually you can move beyond mere fact into significance and speculation—how a new discovery alters what was known, what new avenues of research it might open, where the research might be applied. There's no limit to how wide the inverted pyramid can become, but the reader will understand the broad implications only if he starts with a narrow fact.

A good example is an article that ran on page 1 of the *New York Times,* by Harold M. Schmeck, Jr.

> WASHINGTON—There was a chimpanzee in California with a talent for playing ticktacktoe. Its trainers were delighted with this evidence of learning, but they were even more impressed by something else. They found they could tell from the animal's brain whether any particular move would be right or wrong. It depended on the chimpanzee's state of attention. When the trained animal was properly attentive, he made the right move.

Well, that's a reasonably interesting fact. But why is it worth page 1 of the *Times?* Paragraph 2 tells me:

> The significant fact was that scientists were able to recognize that state. By elaborate computer analysis of brain wave signals they were learning to distinguish what might be called "states of mind."

But hadn't this been possible before?

> This was far more ambitious than simply detecting gross states of arousal, drowsiness or sleep. It was a new step toward understanding how the brain works.

How is it a new step?

The chimpanzee and the research team at the University of California at Los Angeles have graduated from the ticktacktoe stage, but the work with brain waves is continuing. It has already revealed some surprising insights to the brain's behavior during space flight. It shows promise of application to social and domestic problems on earth and even to improvements in human learning.

Good. I could hardly ask a broader application of the research: space, human problems and the cognitive process. But is it an isolated effort? No indeed.

It is part of the large ferment of modern brain research in progress in laboratories throughout the United States and abroad. Involved are all manner of creatures from men and monkeys to rats and mice, goldfish, flatworms and Japanese quail.

I begin to see the total context. But what is the purpose?

The ultimate goal is to understand the human brain—that incredible three-pound package of tissue that can imagine the farthest reaches of the universe and the ultimate core of the atom but cannot fathom its own functioning. Each research project bites off a little piece of an immense puzzle.

So now I know where the chimp at U.C.L.A. fits into the spectrum of international science. Knowing this, I'm ready to go back and learn about his particular contribution.

In the case of the chimpanzee being taught to play ticktacktoe, even the trained eye could see nothing beyond the ordinary in the wavy lines being traced on paper to represent electrical waves from an animal's brain. But through analysis by computer it was possible to tell which traces showed that the animal was about to make the right move and which preceded a mistake.

An important key was the system of computer analysis developed largely by Dr. John Hanley. The state of mind that always foreshadowed a correct answer was one that might be described as trained attentiveness. Without the computer's ability to analyze the huge complexities of the recorded brain waves, the "signatures" of such states could not have been detected.

The article goes on for four columns to describe potential uses of the research—measuring causes of domestic tension, for instance, or reducing the rush-hour stress of drivers—and eventually it touches on work being done in many corners of the world and in various pockets of medicine and psychology. But it started with one chimpanzee playing ticktacktoe.

You can take much of the mystery out of science writing by helping the reader to identify with the scientific work being done. This means, once again, looking for the human element—and if you have to settle for a chimpanzee, at least that's the next-highest rung on the Darwinian ladder.

One obvious human element is yourself. Use your own experience to connect the reader to some mechanism that also touches his life. In the following article on memory and how it operates, which ran in *Life*, note how the writer, Will Bradbury, gives us at the start a personal handle with which to grab an intricate subject:

> Even now I see the dark cloud of sand before it hits my eyes, hear my father's calm voice urging me to cry the sting away, and feel anger and humiliation burn in my chest. More than 30 years have passed since that moment when a playmate, fighting for my toy ambulance, tossed a handful of sand in my face. Yet the

look of the sand and ambulance, the sound of my father's voice and the throb of my bruised feelings all remain sharp and clear today. They are the very first
things I can remember, the first bits of visual, verbal
and emotional glass imbedded in the mosaic I have
come to know as *me* by what is certainly the brain's
most essential function—memory.

Without this miracle function that enables us to store
and recall information, the brain's crucial systems for
waking and sleeping, for expressing how we feel about
things and for performing complicated acts could do little more than fumble with sensory inputs of the moment. Nor would man have a real feeling of self, for he
would have no gallery of the past to examine, learn
from, enjoy and, when necessary, hide away in. Yet
after thousands of years of theorizing, of reading and
misreading his own behavioral quirks, man is just beginning to have some understanding of the mysterious process that permits him to break and store bits of passing
time.

One problem has been to decide what memory is and
what things have it. Linseed oil, for example, has a kind
of memory. Once exposed to light, even if only briefly,
it will change consistency and speed the *second* time it
is exposed. It will "remember" its first encounter with
the light. Electronic and fluidic circuits also have memory of a more sophisticated kind. Built into computers,
they are able to store and retrieve extraordinary
amounts of information. And the human body has at
least four kinds of memory. . . .

That's a fine lead. Who doesn't possess some cluster of
vivid images that he can recall from an inconceivably early
age? The reader is eager to learn how such a feat of storage
and retrieval is accomplished. The example of the linseed oil

is just piquant enough to make us wonder what "memory" really is, and then the writer reverts to the human frame of reference, for it is man who has built the computer circuits and who has four kinds of memory himself.

Another method is to weave a scientific story around someone else. This is the continuing appeal of the articles called "Annals of Medicine" that Berton Roueché has long been writing in *The New Yorker*. They are detective stories, almost always involving a victim—some ordinary person struck by a mystifying ailment—and a gumshoe obsessed with finding the villain. Here's how one of them begins:

> At about 8 o'clock on Monday morning, Sept. 25, 1944, a ragged, aimless old man of 82 collapsed on the sidewalk on Dey Street, near the Hudson Terminal. Innumerable people must have noticed him, but he lay there alone for several minutes, dazed, doubled up with abdominal cramps, and in an agony of retching. Then a policeman came along. Until the policeman bent over the old man he may have supposed that he had just a sick drunk on his hands; wanderers dropped by drink are common in that part of town in the early morning. It was not an opinion that he could have held for long. The old man's nose, lips, ears and fingers were sky-blue.

By noon, eleven blue men have been admitted to nearby hospitals. But never fear—Dr. Ottavio Pellitteri, field epidemiologist, is quickly on the scene and telephoning Dr. Morris Greenberg at the Bureau of Preventable Diseases. Slowly the two men piece together fragments of evidence that seem to defy medical history until the case is at last nailed down and the villain identified as a type of poisoning so rare that many standard texts on toxicology don't even mention it.

Roueché's secret is as old as the art of storytelling. We are in on a chase and a mystery. But he doesn't start with the medical history of poisoning, or talk about standard texts on toxicology. He gives us a man—and not only a man but a blue one.

Another way of helping the reader to understand unfamiliar facts is to relate them to sights that he *is* familiar with. Reduce the abstract principle to an image he can visualize. Moshe Safdie, the architect who conceived Habitat, the innovative housing complex at Montreal's Expo 67, explains in his book, *Beyond Habitat*, that man would build better than he does if he took the time to see how nature does the job, since "nature makes form, and form is a by-product of evolution":

> One can study plant and animal life, rock and crystal formations, and discover the reasons for their particular form. The nautilus has evolved so that when its shell grows, its head will not get stuck in the opening. This is known as gnomonic growth; it results in the spiral formation. It is, mathematically, the only way it can grow.
>
> The same is true of achieving strength with a particular material. Look at the wings of a vulture, at its bone formation. A most intricate three-dimensional geometric pattern has evolved, a kind of space frame, with very thin bones that get thicker at the ends. The main survival problem for the vulture is to develop strength in the wing (which is under tremendous bending movement when the bird is flying) without building up weight, as that would limit its mobility. Through evolution the vulture has the most efficient structure one can imagine—a space frame in bone.

"For each aspect of life there are responses of form," Safdie writes, noting that the maple and the elm have wide leaves to absorb the maximum amount of sun for survival in a temperate climate, whereas the olive tree has a leaf that rotates because it must preserve moisture and can't absorb heat, and the cactus turns itself perpendicular to light. We may not know anything about botany, but we can all picture a maple leaf and a cactus plant. With every hard principle Safdie gives us a simple illustration:

> Economy and survival are the two key words in nature. Examined out of context, the neck of the giraffe seems uneconomically long, but it is economical in view of the fact that most of the giraffe's food is high on the tree. . . . Beauty as we understand it, and as we admire it in nature, is never arbitrary. The color and shape of flowers directly relate to their ability to attract insects; the color and formation of insects relate to their ability to camouflage themselves against the background of flowers.

Another way of making science accessible is to write like a person and not like a scientist. It's the same old question of warmth, of being yourself. Just because you're dealing with a scholarly discipline that's usually reported in a style of dry pedantry is no reason why you shouldn't write in good fresh English. Loren Eiseley is an example of a naturalist who refused to be cowed by nature as he passed on to us—in *The Immense Journey*—not only his knowledge but his enthusiasms:

> I have long been an admirer of the octopus. The cephalopods are very old, and they have slipped, protean, through many shapes. They are the wisest of the mollusks, and I have always felt it to be just as well for us that they never came ashore, but—there are other things that have.
>
> There is no need to be frightened. It is true that some of the creatures are odd, but I find the situation rather heartening than otherwise. It gives one a feeling of confidence to see nature still busy with experiments, still

dynamic, and not through or satisfied because a Devonian fish managed to end as a two-legged character with a straw hat. There are other things brewing and growing in the oceanic vat. It pays to know this. It pays to know there is just as much future as past. The only thing that doesn't pay is to be sure of man's own part in it.

Or take this passage about ants from *The Lives of a Cell,* by Lewis Thomas, a biologist by training but a natural writer. Ants are very low on the list of subjects I want to read about—or so I thought. But Dr. Thomas can get me interested in any subject that interests *him.* What lures me is not the ant; it's the man and his mind.

A solitary ant, afield, cannot be considered to have much of anything on his mind; indeed, with only a few neurons strung together by fibers, he can't be imagined to have a mind at all, much less a thought. He is more like a ganglion on legs. Four ants together, or ten, encircling a dead moth on a path, begin to look more like an idea. They fumble and shove, gradually moving the food toward the Hill, but as though by blind chance. It is only when you watch the dense mass of thousands of ants, crowded together around the Hill, blackening the ground, that you begin to see the whole beast, and now you observe it thinking, planning, calculating. It is an intelligence, a kind of live computer, with crawling bits for its wits.

At a stage in the construction, twigs of a certain size are needed, and all the members forage obsessively for twigs of just this size. Later, when outer walls are to be finished, thatched, the size must change, and as though given orders by telephone, all the workers shift the search to the new twigs. If you disturb the arrangement of a part of the Hill, hundreds of ants will set it vibrating, shifting, until it is put right again. Distant sources of food are somehow sensed, and long lines, like tentacles, reach out over the ground, up over walls, behind boulders, to fetch it in.

I have quoted from so many writers, writing about so many different facets of our physical world, to show that they all come across primarily as people, finding a common thread of humanity between themselves and their specialty and their readers. They all write cleanly and without pretense; they all use vivid images from the vocabulary of everyday life. They aren't scared by their subject. On the contrary, they seem to be relaxed and having a good time. You, too, can achieve this rapport.

Though I have used science as a demonstration model, the same principles apply to any field where the reader must be led across territory that is new and forbidding: business and finance, medicine and public health, government and consumerism, energy and nuclear power, ecology and architecture. Only through clear writing can we affect our future and make educated choices in areas where we have little or no education.

Of all these areas, none is more urgent than the survival of life on earth, and no writer has confronted the problem more lucidly than Freeman Dyson in *Weapons and Hope*. The literature of disarmament falls mainly into two camps: at one extreme it's too technical for the layman to make use of, or, at the other, it's too apocalyptic. Dyson stands in the middle, helpful to everyone. He can explain the most complex nuclear weapons systems and their relative strengths and weaknesses with utmost clarity. But he also knows that our salvation is in the hands of man, not machines, and that we will only survive if we understand the kinds of military and political thinking that have brought us to the edge of extinction and that continue to hold us there:

The concept is called "assured destruction" because of McNamara's choice of words. Assured destruction has at least the virtue of robustness. McNamara never had any difficulty in explaining it to congressional committees. It survived untouched the Vietnam war and the attendant political upheavals which changed so many other aspects of American life and incidentally put an end to McNamara's tenure as secretary of defense. It still survives today as an important component of American strategy and of American conduct of arms control negotiations. The words "assured destruction" are unambiguous and their meaning survives translation into Russian. The ability to survive translation is an essential virtue. Endless trouble and misunderstanding were caused by the word "deterrence," which is a slippery concept in English and which is usually translated into Russian as *ustrashenie*. It turns out that *ustrashenie* really means "intimidation," and so it was not surprising that discussions with Russians about deterrence proved frustrating to all concerned. There is no such difficulty with "assured destruction." Assured destruction means exactly what it says. It means that no matter what you do and no matter what happens to us, we retain the capability to bomb you back into the Stone Age.

16. Professional Writing and Business Writing

Although this is a book about writing, it's not meant just for "writers." Its points are valid for all the people who have to do some writing just to get along in their job. The inter-office memo and the marketing analysis, for instance, are forms of writing, and many a career rises or falls on the ability or inability of an employee to state an idea or a set of facts clearly and concisely.

Most people work for institutions—businesses and banks, insurance firms and law firms, government agencies, school systems, nonprofit organizations and various other entities. Many of them are executives whose writing goes out to the public: the corporation president addressing his stock-holders, the bank manager explaining a change in pro-cedure, the school principal writing a newsletter to parents. Whoever they are, they are so uncomfortable with words, or so fearful, that their sentences lack all humanity—and so do their institutions. In fact, it's hard to imagine that these are real places where real men and women come to work every morning.

But just because people work for an institution they don't have to write like one. Institutions can be warmed up. Ad-ministrators and executives can be turned into human beings. Information can be imparted clearly and without pomposity. It's a question of remembering that readers iden-tify with people, not with abstractions like "profitability," or

with Latinate nouns like "utilization" and "implementation,"
or with inert constructions in which nobody can be visu-
alized doing something ("pre-feasibility studies are in the pa-
perwork stage").

Nowhere has the point been made better than in George
Orwell's "translation" into modern bureaucratic fuzz of this
famous verse from Ecclesiastes:

> I returned and saw under the sun, that the race is not
> to the swift, nor the battle to the strong, neither yet
> bread to the wise, nor yet riches to men of understand-
> ing, nor yet favor to men of skill; but time and chance
> happeneth to them all.

Orwell's version goes:

> Objective consideration of contemporary phenomena
> compels the conclusion that success or failure in com-
> petitive activities exhibits no tendency to be commensu-
> rate with innate capacity, but that a considerable
> element of the unpredictable must invariably be taken
> into account.

First, notice how the two passages look. The one at the
top invites us to read it. The words are short and have air
around them; they convey the rhythms of human speech.
The second one is clotted with long words. It tells us instantly that a ponderous mind is at work. It also tells us that
we don't want to go anywhere with a mind that expresses
itself in such suffocating language. We don't even start reading.

Also notice the content of the two passages. Gone from
the second one are the short words and vivid images from
everyday life—the race and the battle, the bread and the
riches—and in their place have waddled the long and flabby
nouns of generalized meaning. Gone is any sense of what
one person did ("I returned") or what he realized ("saw")

about one of life's central mysteries: the capriciousness of fate.

Let me illustrate how this disease infects our everyday life. I'll use school principals as my first example, not because they are the worst offenders (they aren't), but because I happen to have such an example. My points are intended, however, for all the big and small executives in all the organizations where language has lost its humanity and nobody quite knows what the people in charge are trying to say.

My encounter with the principals began when I got a call from Ernest B. Fleishman, superintendent of schools in Greenwich, Connecticut. "We'd like you to come and 'dejargonize' us," he said. "We don't think we can teach students to write unless all of us at the top of the school system clean up our own writing." He said he would send me some typical materials that had originated within the system. His idea was for me to analyze the writing and then conduct a workshop.

What appealed to me was the willingness of Dr. Fleishman and his colleagues to make themselves vulnerable. We decided on a date, and soon a fat envelope arrived. It contained various internal memos and a number of mimeographed newsletters that had been mailed to parents by the sixteen elementary, junior and senior high schools.

The newsletters had a cheery and informal look. Obviously the system was making an effort to communicate warmly with its families. But even at first glance certain chilly phrases caught my eye—"prioritized evaluative procedures," "modified departmentalized schedule"—and one principal promised that his school would provide "enhanced positive learning environments." Just as obviously the system wasn't communicating as warmly as it thought it was.

I studied the principals' material and divided it into good and bad examples. On the appointed morning in Greenwich I found forty principals, directors and curriculum coordinators assembled and eager to learn. I said I could only applaud them for submitting to a process that so threatened their identity. In the national clamor over why Johnny can't write, Dr. Fleishman was the first adult in my experience who admitted that youth has no monopoly on verbal sludge and that the problem must also be attacked at the top.

I told the principals that as parents we want to think of the men and women who run our children's schools as people not unlike ourselves. We are suspicious of pretentiousness, of all the fad words that the social scientists have coined to avoid the horrid necessity of making themselves clear to ordinary mortals. I urged them to be natural. How we write and how we talk is how we define ourselves.

I asked them to listen to how they were defining themselves to the community. I had made forty copies of certain bad examples, changing the names of the schools and principals. I explained that I would read some of the examples aloud. Later we would see if they could turn what they had written into plain English. This was my first example:

Dear Parent:

We have established a special phone communication system to provide additional opportunities for parent input. During this year we will give added emphasis to the goal of communication and utilize a variety of means to accomplish this goal. Your inputs, from the unique position as a parent, will help us to plan and implement an educational plan that meets the needs of your child. An open dialogue, feedback and sharing of information between parents and teachers will enable us to work with your child in the most effective manner.

Dr. George B. Jones
Principal

That's the kind of communication I don't want to receive,

unique though my parent inputs might be. I'd like to be told that the school is going to make it easier for me to telephone the teachers and that they hope I'll call often to discuss how my children are getting along. Instead the parent gets junk: "special phone communication system," "added emphasis to the goal of communication," "plan and implement an educational plan." As for "open dialogue, feedback and sharing of information," they are three ways of saying the same thing.

Dr. Jones is clearly a man who means well, and his plan is one that we all want: a chance to pick up the phone and tell the principal what a great kid Johnny is despite that unfortunate incident in the playground last Tuesday. But Dr. Jones doesn't sound like a person I want to call. In fact, he doesn't sound like a person. His message could have been tapped out by a computer. He is squandering a rich resource: himself.

Another example that I chose was a "Principal's Greeting" sent to parents at the start of the year. It consisted of two paragraphs that were very different:

> Fundamentally, Foster is a good school. Pupils who require help in certain subjects or study skills areas are receiving special attention. In the school year ahead we seek to provide enhanced positive learning environments. Children, and staff, must work in an atmosphere that is conducive to learning. Wide varieties of instructional materials are needed. Careful attention to individual abilities and learning styles is required. Cooperation between school and home is extremely important to the learning process. All of us should be aware of desired educational objectives for every child.
>
> Keep informed about what is planned for our children this year and let us know about your own questions and about any special needs your child may have. I have met many of you in the first few weeks. Please continue

to stop in to introduce yourself or to talk about Foster. I look forward to a very productive year for all of us.

Dr. Ray B. Dawson
Principal

In the second paragraph I'm being greeted by a person; in the first I'm hearing from an educator. I like the real Dr. Dawson of Paragraph 2. He talks in warm and comfortable phrases: "Keep informed," "let us know," "I have met," "Please continue," "I look forward."

By contrast, Educator Dawson of Paragraph 1 never uses "I" or even suggests a sense of "I." He falls back on the jargon of his profession, where he feels safe, not stopping to notice that he really isn't telling the parent anything. What are "study skills areas" and how do they differ from "subjects"? What are "enhanced positive learning environments" and how do they differ from "an atmosphere that is conducive to learning"? What are "wide varieties of instructional materials": pencils, textbooks, filmstrips? What exactly are "learning styles"? What "educational objectives" are "desired," and who desires them?

The second paragraph, in short, is warm and personal; the other is pedantic and vague. This was a pattern that I found repeatedly. Whenever the principals wrote to notify the parents of some human detail they wrote with humanity:

> It seems that traffic is beginning to pile up again in front of the school. If you can possibly do so, please come to the rear of the school for your child at the end of the day.

> I would appreciate it if you would speak with your children about their behavior in the cafeteria. Many of you would be totally dismayed if you could observe the manners of your children while they are eating. Check

occasionally to see if they owe money for lunch. Sometimes children are very slow in repaying.

But when the educators wrote to explain how they proposed to do their educating, they vanished without a trace:

> In this document you will find the program goals and objectives that have been identified and prioritized. Evaluative procedures for the objectives were also established based on acceptable criteria.

> Prior to the implementation of the above practice, students were given very little exposure to multiple choice questions. It is felt that the use of practice questions correlated to the unit that a student is presently studying has had an extremely positive effect as the test scores confirm.

After I had read various good and bad examples, the principals began to hear the difference between their true selves and their educator selves. The problem was how to close the gap. I recited my articles of faith: humanity, clarity, simplicity, vitality. I explained about using active verbs and avoiding windy nouns. I told them not to use the private vocabulary of education as a crutch. There is almost no subject that can't be made accessible in good English.

These were all basic tenets, but the principals wrote them down as if they had never heard them before—and maybe they hadn't, or at least not for many years. Perhaps this is why bureaucratic prose becomes so turgid, whatever the bureaucracy. Once an administrator rises to a certain level, nobody ever points out to him again the beauty of a simple declarative sentence, or shows him how his writing has become swollen with ornate generalizations.

Finally our workshop got down to work. I distributed my forty copies and asked the principals to rewrite the more knotty sentences. It was a grim moment. They had met the enemy for the first time. They scribbled on their pads and scratched out what they had scribbled. Some didn't write anything. Some crumpled their paper. They began, in fact, to look like writers. An awful silence hung over the room, broken only by the crossing out of sentences and the crumpling of paper. They began to sound like writers.

As the day went on, they slowly relaxed. They began to write in the first person and to use active verbs. For a while they still couldn't loose their grip on long words and vague nouns ("parent communication response"). But gradually their sentences became human. When I asked them to tackle "Evaluative procedures for the objectives were also established based on acceptable criteria," one of them wrote: "At the end of the year we will evaluate our progress." Another wrote: "We will see how well we have succeeded."

That's the kind of plain talk that a parent wants. It's also what the stockholder wants from his corporation, what the customer wants from his bank, what the widow wants from the government office that is handling her social security. There is a yearning for human contact and a resentment of bombast. Any institution that won't take the trouble in its writing to be both clear and personal will lose friends, customers and money. Let me put it another way for business executives: a shortfall will be experienced in anticipated profitability.

Here's an example of how organizations throw away their humanity with pompous language. It's a "customer bulletin" distributed by a major corporation. The sole purpose of a customer bulletin is to give helpful information to a customer. This one begins: "Companies are increasingly turning to capacity planning techniques to determine when future processing loads will exceed processing capabilities." That sentence is no favor to the customer; it's congealed with Orwellian nouns like "capacity" and "capabilities" that have no specific procedures that the customer can picture. What *are* capacity planning techniques? Whose capacity is being planned? By whom? The second sentence says: "Capacity planning adds objectivity to the decision-making process." More pompous nouns. The third sentence says: "Management is given enhanced decision participation in key areas of information system resources."

The customer has to stop after every sentence and translate it. The bulletin might as well be in French. He starts with the first sentence—the one about capacity planning techniques. Translated, that means "It helps to know when you're giving your computer more than it can handle." The second sentence—"Capacity planning adds objectivity to the decision-making process"—means that you should know the facts before you decide. The third sentence—the one about enhanced decision participation—means "The more you know about your system the better it will work." It could also mean several other things.

But the customer isn't going to keep translating much longer. Soon he's going to start looking for another company. He thinks: "If these guys are so smart, why can't they tell me what they do? Maybe they're *not* so smart." The bulletin goes on to say that "for future cost avoidance, productivity has been enhanced." That seems to mean that the product will be free: all costs have been avoided. Next the bulletin assures the customer that "the system is delivered with functionality." That means it works. I should hope so.

Finally, at the end, we get a glimmer of humanity. The writer of the bulletin asks a satisfied customer why he chose this system. The man says he chose it because of the company's reputation for service. He says: "A computer is like a sophisticated pencil. You don't care how it works, but if it breaks you want someone there to fix it." Notice how refreshing that sentence is after all the garbage that preceded it: in its language (comfortable words), in its details that we can visualize (the pencil), and above all in its humanity. The writer has taken the coldness out of a complex technology by relating it to a process that we're all familiar with—waiting for the repairman to come when something breaks.

Still, plain talk will not be easily achieved in corporate America. Too much vanity is on the line. Executives and managers at every level are prisoners of the notion that a simple style reflects a simple mind. Actually a simple style is the result of hard work and hard thinking; a muddled style reflects a muddled thinker or a person too dumb or too lazy to organize his thoughts. Remember that what you write is often the only chance you'll get to present yourself to someone whose business you want. If what you write is ornate or pompous or fuzzy, that's how you'll be perceived.

I learned about corporate America by venturing out into it, after Greenwich, to conduct similar workshops for some of the country's biggest corporations, which also asked to be dejargonized. "We don't even understand our own memos anymore," they told me. I worked with the men and women who write the vast amounts of material that these companies generate for internal and external consumption. The internal material consists of house organs and newsletters whose purpose is to tell employees what's happening at their "facility" and to give them a sense of belonging. The external material includes the glossy magazines and annual reports that go to stockholders, the speeches that are delivered by high executives, the releases that are sent to the press and the consumer manuals that explain how the product works. I found almost all of it lacking in human juices and much of it impenetrable.

Typical of the sentences in the newsletters was this one:

Announced concurrently with the above enhancements were changes to the System Support Program, a program product which operates in conjunction with the

NCP. Among the additional functional enhancements
are dynamic reconfiguration and inter-systems com-
munications.

There's no joy for the writer in such work, and certainly
none for the reader. It's language out of *Star Trek*, and if I
were an employee I would not be cheered—or informed—
by these efforts to raise my morale. In fact, I would soon
stop reading them. I told the corporate writers that they had
to find the people behind the fine achievements that were
being described. "Go to the engineer who conceived the
new system," I said, "or to the designer who designed it, or
to the technician who assembled it, and get them to tell you
in their own words how the idea came to them, or how they
put it together, or how it will be used by real people out in
the real world." The way to warm up any institution is to
locate the missing "I." He or she is the most interesting part
of any story.

The writers explained that they often did interview the
engineer but couldn't get him to talk English. They showed
me some typical quotations in their newsletters that proved
the point all too well. The engineers spoke in an arcane language studded with acronyms ("Sub-system support is available only with VSAG or TNA"). I said that the writers had to
keep going back to the engineer until he finally made himself intelligible. They said that the engineer didn't *want* to
be made intelligible: if he spoke too simply he would look
like a jerk to his peers. I said that their responsibility was to
the facts and to the reader, not to the vanity of the engineer.
I urged them to believe in themselves as writers and not to
relinquish control. They replied that this was easier said
than done in hierarchical corporations where approval is required at various higher levels. I sensed an undercurrent of
fear: do things the company way and don't risk your job trying to make the company human.

But I found that high executives were equally victimized by the syndrome of sounding important. One corporation, for instance, had a monthly newsletter to enable "management" to share its concerns with middle managers and lower employees. Prominent in every issue was a message of exhortation from the division vice-president, whom I'll call Vernon Smith. Judging by his monthly message, he was a pompous ass, saying nothing and saying it in inflated verbiage.

When I mentioned this, the writers said that Vernon Smith was actually a diffident man and a good executive with a good mind. They pointed out that he doesn't write the message himself; it's written for him. I said that Vernon Smith was being done a disservice—that the writers should go to him every month (with a tape recorder, if necessary) and stay there until he talked about his concerns in the same language that he would use when he got home and talked to Mrs. Vernon Smith.

What I realized—by extension—was that most executives in America don't write what appears over their signature or what they say in their speeches. They have surrendered the qualities that make them unique. If they and their institutions seem cold and pretentious it's because they acquiesce in the process of being pumped up and dried out. Preoccupied with their complex equipment, they forget that some of the most powerful tools they possess—for good and for bad—are words.

If you work for an institution, whatever your job, whatever your level, be yourself when you write. You will stand out as a real person among the robots, and your example might even persuade Vernon Smith to write his own stuff.

17. Sports

I learned about the circuit clout before I learned about the electrical circuit. I also learned early—as a child addict of the sports pages—that a hurler (or twirler) who faces left when he toes the slab is a southpaw or a portsider. Southpaws were always lanky, portsiders always chunky, though I've never heard "chunky" applied to anything else except peanut butter (to distinguish it from "creamy") and I have no idea what a chunky person would look like. When hurlers fired the old horsehide, a batsman would try to solve their slants. If he succeeded he might rap a sharp bingle to the outfield, garnering a win for the home contingent, or at least knotting the count. If not, he might bounce into a twin killing, snuffing out a rally and dimming his team's hopes in the flag scramble.

I could go on, mining every sport for its lingo and extracting from the mother lode a variety of words found nowhere else in the mother tongue. Do we ever "garner" anything except a win? I could write of hoopsters and pucksters, grapplers and matmen, strapping oarsmen and gridiron standouts. I could rhapsodize about the old pigskin—far more passionately than any pig farmer—or describe the frenzied bleacherites caught up in the excitement of the autumn classic. I could, in short, write in sports English instead of good English, as if they were two different languages. Of course they're not. As in the case of writing about science or any other special subject, there's no substitute for the best.

What, you might ask, is wrong with "southpaw"? Shouldn't we be grateful for the addition to our language of a word so picturesque? Why isn't it a relief to have twirlers and circuit clouts instead of the same old pitchers and home runs? The answer is that these words have become even cheaper currency than the coins they were meant to replace. They come flooding automatically out of the typewriter of every scribe (sportswriter) in every pressbox.

The man who first thought of "southpaw" had a right to be pleased. I like to think that he allowed himself the small smile that is the due of anyone who invents a good novelty. But how long ago was that? The color that "southpaw" added to the language has paled with decades of repetition, along with the hundreds of other idioms that now form the fabric of daily sportswriting. There is a weariness about them that leaves us numb. We read the articles to find out who won, and how, but we don't read them with any real enjoyment.

The best sportswriters know this. They avoid the exhausted synonyms and strive for freshness elsewhere in the construction of a sentence. You can search the columns of Red Smith and never find a batsman bouncing into a twin killing. Smith was never afraid to let a batter hit into a double play. But you will find hundreds of unusual words—good English words—chosen with precision and fitted into situations where no other sportswriter would put them. They gratify us because the writer obviously cared about using fresh imagery in a field where his competitors settled for the same old stuff. That's why Red Smith was still king of his field after more than half a century of writing, and why his competitors had long since been sent—as they would be the first to say—to the showers.

Across the years I remember countless phrases in Red Smith's columns that took me by surprise with their humor and originality. It was a pleasure to read about a quarterback who was "scraped off the turf like apple butter." I remember countless times when Smith, a devout angler, baited his hook and came up with that slippery fish, a sports commissioner, gasping for air.

"In most professional sports the bottom has just about dropped out of the czar business," he wrote in 1971, noting once again that the cupidity of team owners has a tendency to outrun the courage of the sport's monitors. "The first and toughest of the overlords was Kenesaw Mountain Landis, who came to power in 1920 and ruled with a heavy hand until his death in 1944. But if baseball started with Little Caesar, it wound up with Ethelred the Unready." Red Smith was the daily guardian of our perspective, a writer who kept us honest. But that was largely because he was writing good English. His style was not only graceful but strong enough to carry strong convictions.

What keeps the average writer from writing good English is, first, the misapprehension that he shouldn't be trying to. He has been reared on so much jargon, so many clichés, that he thinks they are the required tools of the trade.

He is also obsessed by synonyms. He has a dread of repeating the word that's easiest for the reader to visualize— batter, runner, golfer, boxer—if a synonym can be found. And usually, with exertion, it can. This excerpt from a college newspaper is typical:

> Bob Hornsby extended his skein yesterday by toppling Dartmouth's Jerry Smithers, 6–4, 6–2, to lead the netmen to victory over a surprisingly strong foe. The gangling junior put his big serve to good use in keeping the Green captain off balance. The Memphis native was in top form as he racked up the first four games, breaking the Indian's service twice in the first four games. The Exeter graduate faltered and the Hanover mainstay

rallied to cop three games. But the racquet ace was not
to be denied, and the Yankee's attempt to knot the first
stanza at 4–4 failed when he was passed by a cross-court
volley on the sixth deuce point. The redhead was simply
too determined, and . . .

What ever became of Bob Hornsby? (Or, for that matter,
Jerry Smithers?) Well might you ask. Hornsby has been
metamorphosed within one paragraph into the gangling
junior, the Memphis native, the Exeter graduate, the racquet ace and the redhead. The reader doesn't know him in
these various disguises—or care. He only wants the clearest
picture of what happened. Never be afraid to repeat the
player's name and to keep the details of the game simple. A
set or an inning doesn't have to be recycled into a stanza or a
frame just to avoid redundancy. The cure is worse than the
ailment.

Another obsession is with numbers. True, every sports addict lives with a head full of statistics, cross-filed for ready
access, and many a baseball fan who once flunked simple
arithmetic can perform prodigies of instant calculation in the
ball park on a summer afternoon. Still, some statistics are
more important than others. If a pitcher wins his twentieth
game, if a golfer shoots a 61, if a runner runs the mile in
3:48, please mention it. But don't get carried away:

AUBURN, Ala., Nov. 1 (UPI)—Pat Sullivan, Auburn's
sophomore quarterback, scored two touchdowns and
passed for two today to hand Florida a 38–12 defeat, the
first of the season for the ninth-ranked Gators.

John Reaves of Florida broke two Southeastern Conference records and tied another. The tall sophomore
from Tampa, Fla., gained 369 yards passing, pushing
his six-game season total to 2,115. That broke the
S.E.C. season record of 2,012 set by the 1966 Heisman
trophy winner, in 10 games.

Reaves attempted 66 passes—an S.E.C. record—and tied the record of 33 completions set this fall by Mississippi's Archie Manning.

Fortunately for Auburn, nine of Reaves's passes were intercepted—breaking the S.E.C. record of eight interceptions suffered by Georgia's Zeke Bratkowski against Georgia Tech in 1951.

Reaves's performance left him only a few yards short of the S.E.C. season total offense record of 2,187 set by Georgia's Frank Sinkwich in 11 games in 1942. And his two touchdown passes against Auburn left him only one touchdown pass short of the S.E.C. season record of 23 set in 1950 by Kentucky's Babe Parilli. . . .

Those are the first five paragraphs of a six-paragraph story that was prominently displayed in my New York newspaper, a long way from Auburn. It has a certain mounting hilarity—a figure freak amok at his typewriter. But can anybody read it? And does anybody care? Only Zeke Bratkowski—finally off the hook.

Sports is one of the richest fields now open to the nonfiction writer. Many authors better known for "serious" books have done some of their most solid work as observers of athletic combat. John McPhee's *Levels of the Game* and George Plimpton's *Paper Lion*—one a book about tennis, the other about professional football—take us deeply into the lives of the players. In mere detail they have enough information to keep any fan happy. But what makes them special is their humanity. Who is this strange bird, the winning athlete, and what engines keep him going?

One of the classics in the literature of baseball is John Updike's account of Ted Williams' final game, on September 28, 1960. The article builds to the almost mythical moment in the eighth inning when the forty-two-year-old "Kid," coming up for his last time at bat in Fenway Park, hits one

over the wall. But before that Updike has compressed much
of the career of "this brittle and temperamental player" in
one paragraph that is as graceful as Williams' own swing:

I remember watching one of his home runs from the
bleachers of Shibe Park; it went over the first baseman's
head and rose meticulously along a straight line and was
still rising when it cleared the fence. The trajectory
seemed qualitatively different from anything anyone
else might hit. For me, Williams is the classic ballplayer
of the game on a hot August weekday, before a small
crowd, when the only thing at stake is the tissue-thin
difference between a thing done well and a thing done
ill. Baseball is a game of the long season, of relentless
and gradual averaging-out. Irrelevance—since the reference point of most individual games is remote and sta-
tistical—always threatens its interest, which can be
maintained not by the occasional heroics that sportswriters feed upon but by players who always care; who care,
that is to say, about themselves and their art. Insofar as
the clutch hitter is not a sportswriter's myth, he is a
vulgarity, like a writer who writes only for money. It
may be that, compared to managers' dreams, such as
Joe DiMaggio and the always helpful Stan Musial, Williams is an icy star. But of all team sports, baseball, with
its graceful intermittences of action, its immense and
tranquil field sparsely settled with poised men in white,
its dispassionate mathematics, seems to me best suited
to accommodate, and be ornamented by, a loner. It is
essentially a lonely game. No other player visible to my
generation has concentrated within himself so much of
the sport's poignance, has so assiduously refined his natural skills, has so constantly brought to the plate that
intensity of competence that crowds the throat with joy.

What gives this passage its depth is that it's the work of a writer, not a sportswriter. Updike knows there's not much more to say about Williams' matchless ability at the plate: the famous swing, the eyes that could see the stitches on a baseball arriving at ninety miles an hour. But the mystery of the man is still unsolved, even on the final day of his career, and that's where Updike steers our attention, suggesting that baseball was suited to such a reclusive star because it's a lonely game. The very idea takes us by surprise. Baseball lonely? Our great American tribal rite? Think about it, Updike says.

Something in Updike made contact with something in Williams: two solitary craftsmen laboring in the glare of the crowd. Always look for this human contact. Remember that athletes aren't like ordinary mortals in their relationship to the reader. They are men and women who become part of our lives during the season, almost part of the family, acting out our dreams or filling some other need for us, and we want that bond to be honored. Hold the hype and give us heroes who are believable.

Even Babe Ruth has been ushered down from the sanitized slopes of Olympus and converted into a real person, with appetites as big as his girth, in Robert Creamer's fine biography *Babe*. "The Legend Comes Alive," says the book's subtitle, which is certainly what Ruth would have wanted, hard though the facts may be on those who would like him to stay legendary. The same qualities have gone into Creamer's latest book, *Stengel*. Ten years ago readers might have settled for the standard version of Casey Stengel as an aging pantaloon who mangled the language and somehow managed to win ten pennants. Creamer's Stengel is far more interesting: a complex and serious man who was nobody's fool and whose story is deeply entwined with the history of baseball itself.

Honest portraiture is only one of many realities that have come crowding into what was a simple fairy-tale world.

Sport, in fact, has become one of the liveliest frontiers of social change in America, and good writers will keep watch there and bring the news to the rest of us. Consider the shift in attitudes and values, for instance, that has allowed women reporters to enter the holiest of male temples, the locker room. Roger Angell, a thoughtful writer who never forgets that the appeal of the game lies in its delicate balance of intangibles, gets quickly and compassionately to the heart of the dilemma in *Late Innings:*

> Women in the clubhouse is an emotional issue, almost a parade float of classical postures in which noble-visaged representations of Propriety, Wholesome Sports and the Innocence of the Family are seen to be under attack by similarly admirable figures representing Social Mobility, Equal Opportunity and Freedom of the Press. . . .
>
> The male sportswriters are concerned about the possibility that Commissioner Kuhn's edict [restricting access] will lead to severe limitations on their own rights and long habits of access to ballplayers—specifically, on their being able to talk to them in the clubhouse immediately after the last out, when the sweaty, beer-gulping young participants are fresh in their memories of the game, and their reactions (exultant or despondent, bitter or comical or evasive) may be taken down or taped or translated at once into the heart of the next edition's story or column or sidebar on the game.
>
> Women sportswriters have the same concern, but they have sharper and more personal feelings of anxiety. Almost all of them have encountered the closed locker room door, in baseball and in other sports, and the professional leagues that have reversed themselves and opened some of the clubhouses—notably the National Basketball Association and the National Hockey League—have done so only after prolonged skirmishing with a few vehement

pioneering women writers and their editors. For the most
part, women reporters have had to cajole individual players into emerging, half dressed or clutching a towel, for a
fragmentary interview in a corridor or an equipment
room, or have had to wait outside the door interminably,
dying by inches as a deadline crept closer, until the players emerged, combed and dressed, homeward- or hotel-
ward-bound, and often sucked dry of news by multiple
interviews—and then have had to beg them to summon
up again the now receding contest.

Another new element is high finance. Today I often open
the sports section and think I've stumbled into the business
pages by mistake. Million-dollar contracts swim before my
eyes, replete with bonuses, deferred payments and an-
nuities, many of them extending beyond the year 2000.
Agents and lawyers have elbowed the athletes off the page;
the talk is of lucre and television rights. Big money in turn
has brought big emotional trouble. Reading the sports section is like reading Ann Landers. The game is secondary;
first we have to learn which player's feelings are hurt because the fans are booing him because he's getting $1.9 mil-
lion and only batting .231. In once-sedate tennis the pot of
gold is now enormous and the players are strung as tightly as
their racquets. In football and basketball the pay is sky-high,
and so is the umbrage.

"It wasn't my idea for basketball to become tax-shelter
show biz," Bill Bradley writes in *Life on the Run*, a chronicle
of his seasons with the New York Knicks. Bradley's book is
one of the best examples of the new sportswriting because it
ponders the darker forces that are altering the quality of
American sport—the greed of entrepreneurs, the worship of
stars, the inability to accept defeat:

After Van's departure I realized that no matter how
kind, friendly and genuinely interested the owners may

be, in the end most players are little more than de-
preciable assets to them.

Self-definition comes from external sources, not from
within. While their physical skill lasts, professional athletes are celebrities—fondled and excused, praised and
believed. Only toward the end of their careers do the
stars realize that their sense of identity is insufficient.

The winning team, like the conquering army, claims
everything in its path and seems to say that only winning is important. Yet victory has very narrow meanings
and can become a destructive force. The taste of defeat
has a richness of experience all its own.

Bradley's book is also an excellent travel journal, catching
the fatigue and loneliness of the professional athlete's
nomadic life—the countless night flights and bus rides, the
dreary days and endless waits in motel rooms and terminals:

In the airports that have become our commuter sta-
tions we see so many dramatic personal moments that
we are calloused. To some, we live romantic lives. To
me, every day is a struggle to stay in touch with life's
subtleties.

American sport has always been interwoven with social
history, and the best sportswriters are those who make the
connection. A small but pleasant example of making the connection was a small but pleasant piece by Jean Shepherd
about the Indianapolis 500. The article, which ran in the
New York Times, explains that the Indy has only one coun-
terpart in American sport—the Kentucky Derby—and that
both "can only be understood by the outsider in terms of
folklore":

Any horse that wins the Derby enters the pearly
gates of history forever. Hundreds of horses have won

"classics" over the years, but even non-horseplayers remember Derby winners. So it is with the 500. Who knows or cares what other races Wilbur Shaw might have won in his great career? The fact that he took the 500 three times makes him immortal.

Why the Derby when there are other, richer races? A little history helps. Kentucky, with its great plantations, its soft rolling hills and lazy summers, was the true horse country of America, and 100 years ago when the Derby was born it pitted one aristocratic horse against the other. It was not just another race, but something that came out of the air and the land and the people who lived on it. . . .

Indiana in the early days was to the automobile as Kentucky was and is to the horse. Some of the truly great machines by any world standard were born and bred on the Indiana flatlands. The stylish and terrifying Dusenbergs created by the almost mythical Dusenberg brothers, Fred and August, were hammered out a few miles from the brick track. The Auburn, the Cord and the great racing Studebakers were all spawned in dusty Indiana hamlets and came together every spring in the dawn of automobiling to battle it out.

The automobile also means much more to the common people of the great plains than it does to the city folk who huddle jammed together in the great urban East. It meant, and still means, freedom, mobility and, above all, a way out for lives that are often as monotonous as the landscape they are lived in.

These are the values to look for when you write about sport—people, places, the link between past and present, the tug of the future. Observe closely. Hang around the track and the paddock, the ball park and the rink. Interview in depth. Listen to old-timers. Ponder the changes. Write well.

18. Criticism

Every writer wants at some time to be a critic. The small-town reporter dreams of the moment when his editor will summon him to cover the Russian ballet troupe, the concert pianist, the touring repertory company that has been booked into the local auditorium. Then he will trot out all the hard-won words of his college education—"intuit" and "sensibility" and "Kafkaesque"—and show the whole county that he knows a *glissando* from an *entrechat*. He will discern more symbolism in Ibsen than Ibsen ever thought of.

This is part of the urge. Criticism is the stage on which journalists do their fanciest strutting.

It is also where reputations for wit are born. The American vernacular is rich in epigrams ("She ran the gamut of emotions from A to B") minted by people like Dorothy Parker and George S. Kaufman, who became famous partly by minting them, and the temptation to make an instant name at the expense of some talentless ham is too strong for all but the most saintly.

Not that the epigrams aren't enjoyable. I particularly like Kaufman's hint that Raymond Massey in *Abe Lincoln in Illinois* was perhaps overplaying the title role: "Massey won't be satisfied until he's assassinated." But true wit is rare, and a thousand barbed arrows fall at the feet of the archer for every one that flies. It's also too facile an approach if you want to write serious criticism, for, by no accident, the only epigrams that have survived are cruel ones. It is far easier to bury Caesar than to praise him—and that goes for Cleopatra too. But to say why you think a play is *good*, in words that don't sound banal, is one of the hardest chores in the business.

So don't be deluded that criticism is an easy route to glory. Nor does the job carry as much power as is widely supposed. Probably only the daily drama critic of the *New York Times* can make or break the product—a new play—and a music critic has almost no power at all, writing, as he does, about a cluster of sounds that have vanished into the air and will never be heard in quite the same way again. As for literary critics, they have never kept the best-seller list from becoming a nesting ground for authors like Harold Robbins and Judith Krantz—whose sensibility they don't intuit—and movie critics wield almost no influence except in the case of a foreign film, where a good review can lengthen its run.

A distinction should therefore be made between a "critic" and a "reviewer." In general a reviewer writes for a newspaper or a popular magazine, and what he covers is not primarily an art but an industry—the output of, for instance, the television industry, the motion-picture industry and, increasingly, the publishing industry in its outpouring of "gift books," cookbooks, how-to books, sex books, and other such items of merchandise.

As a reviewer your job is more to report than to make an aesthetic judgment. You are the deputy for the average man or woman who wants to know: "What is the new TV series about?" "Is the movie too dirty for the kids?" "Will the book really improve my sex life or tell me how to make a chocolate mousse?" Think what *you* would want to know if *you* had to spend the money for the movie, the baby-sitter and the long-promised dinner at a good restaurant. Obviously you will make your review simpler and less sophisticated than if you were criticizing a new novel by Thomas Pynchon.

And yet I suggest several conditions that apply equally to good reviewing and good criticism.

One is that a critic should like—or, better still, love—the medium he is reviewing. If you think movies are dumb, don't write about them. The reader deserves a lifelong movie buff who will bring with him a reservoir of knowledge, passion and prejudice. I don't mean that the critic has to like every film. On the contrary, his prejudices are as important as his passions—criticism, after all, is only one person's opinion and a highly subjective form. But he should go to every movie wanting to like it. If he is more often disappointed than pleased, it's because the film has failed to live up to what he knows are its best possibilities. This is far different from the critic who prides himself on hating everything, who relishes giving us his weekly dose of bile. He becomes tiresome faster than you can say "Kafkaesque."

Another rule is: Don't give away too much of the plot. Tell the reader just enough to let him decide whether it's the kind of story he tends to enjoy, but not so much that you will kill his eventual enjoyment. One sentence will often do the trick. "This is a picture about a whimsical Irish priest who enlists the help of three orphan boys dressed as leprechauns to haunt a village where a mean widow has hidden a crock of gold coins." I couldn't be flailed into seeing that movie—I've had my fill of "the little people" on stage and screen. But there are legions who don't share that particular crotchet of mine and would flock to the film. Don't spoil their pleasure by revealing every twist of the narrative—especially the funny part about the troll under the bridge.

A third principle is to use as much specific detail as possible. This avoids dealing in generalities, which, being generalities, mean nothing. "The play is always fascinating" is a typical critic's sentence. But *how* is it fascinating? Your idea of fascinating is different from the reader's. Cite a few examples and let him weigh them on his own fascination scale. Here are excerpts from two separate reviews of a film directed by Joseph Losey. (1) "In its attempts to be civilized and restrained it denies its possibilities for vulgarity and mistakes bloodlessness for taste." The sentence is vague, giving us at the most a whiff of the movie's mood but no image that we can visualize. (2) "Losey pursues a style that finds portents in lampshades and meanings in table settings." The sentence is precise—we know just what kind of arty filmmaking this is. We can almost see the camera lingering with studied sluggishness over the family crystal.

In book reviewing this means allowing the author's words to do their own documentation. Don't say, for instance, that Tom Wolfe's style is gaudy and unusual. Quote a few of his gaudy and unusual sentences and let the reader see how distinctive they are, how quirky. In reviewing a play, don't just tell us that the set is "striking." Describe its various levels, or how it is ingeniously lit, or how it helps the actors to make their entrances and exits as a less imaginative set would not. Put the reader in your theater seat. Help him to see what you saw.

A final caution is to avoid the ecstatic adjectives that occupy such disproportionate space in every critic's quiver—words like "enthralling" and "luminous." Good criticism needs a lean and vivid style to express what you observed and what you think. Florid adjectives smack of the panting prose with which *Vogue* likes to disclose its latest chichi discovery: "We've just heard about the most utterly enchanting little beach at Cozumel."

So much for reviewing and the simpler rules of the game. What, then, is criticism?

Criticism is a serious intellectual act. It tries to appraise serious works of art and to place them in the context of what has been done before in that medium or by that particular artist. This doesn't mean that the critic must limit himself to the work of men and women whose aims are high; he may select some commercial product like *Dynasty* to make a point about American taste and values. But on the whole he doesn't want to waste his time on peddlers. He sees himself as a scholar, and what interests him is the play of ideas in his field.

Therefore if you want to be a critic, steep yourself in the literature of the medium that you hope to make your province. If your goal is to be a theater critic, see every possible play—the good and the bad, the old and the new. Catch up on the past by reading the classics or seeing them in revival. Know your Shakespeare and Shaw, your Chekhov and Molière, your Arthur Miller and Tennessee Williams, and know what they meant to audiences of their era and how they broke new ground. Know the history of the American musical: the distinctive contribution of Jerome Kern and the Gershwin brothers, of Cole Porter, of Rodgers and Hart and Hammerstein, of Frank Loesser and Stephen Sondheim, of Agnes de Mille and Jerome Robbins. Learn everything you can about the great actors and directors and how their methods differed, and about the great clowns like Bert Lahr. Only then can you place every new drama within an older tradition, recognize genius when it comes along and tell the pioneer from the imitator.

I could make the same kind of list for every art. A film critic who reviews a new Fellini picture without having seen Fellini's earlier films is not much help to the serious moviegoer. A music critic should know not only his Bach and Palestrina, his Mozart and Beethoven, but his Schoenberg and Satie, his Ives and Varèse—the theoreticians and mavericks and electronic experimenters.

Obviously I am now also assuming a more urbane body of readers. As a critic you can presuppose certain shared areas of knowledge with the men and women you are writing for.

You don't have to tell them that William Faulkner was a Southern novelist. What you *do* have to do, if you are assessing the first novel of a Southern author and weighing Faulkner's influence, is to generate a provocative idea and to throw it onto the page where your fellow scholars can savor it. They may disagree with your point—that's part of their intellectual fun. But at least they have enjoyed the turn of your mind and the journey that took you to your conclusion. We like a good critic as much for his personality as for his opinions.

Let me take you journeying with a great film critic, James Agee, as he reveals what he liked best about Laurence Olivier's *Henry V.*

Some people, using I wonder what kind of dry ice for comfort, insist that *Henry V* is relatively uninteresting Shakespeare. [But] after hearing it, in this production, I find it as hard to judge fairly even the best writing since Shakespeare as it is to see the objects in a room after looking into the sun.

The one great glory of the film is this language. The greatest credit I can assign to those who made the film is that they have loved and served the language so well. I don't feel that much of the delivery is inspired; it is merely so good, so right, that the words set loose in the graciously designed world of the screen, like so many uncaged birds, fully enjoy and take care of themselves. Neither of the grimmest Shakespearean vices is indulged: none of the text is read in that human, down-to-earth, poetry-is-only-hopped-up-prose manner which is doubtless only proper when a charter subscriber to *PM* reads the [Max] Lerner editorial to his shop-wise fellow traveler; nor is any of it intoned in the nobler manner, as if by a spoiled deacon celebrating the Black Mass down a section of sewerpipe. Most of it is merely spo-

ken by people who know and love poetry as poetry and
have spent a lifetime learning how to speak it accordingly. Their voices, faces and bodies are all in the
charge of a man who has selected them as shrewdly as a
good orchestrator selects and blends his instruments;
and he combines and directs them as a good conductor
conducts an orchestral piece. It is, in fact, no surprise to
learn that Mr. Olivier is fond of music. Charming as it is
to look at, the film is essentially less visual than musical.

Most of us remember *Henry V* for its beauty, its color, its
robust vitality. Agee reminds us that it was built on still stur-
dier pillars. He also tells us a great deal about himself. How
could we not take pleasure in a mind both so finely tuned to
poetry and so impatient with the grandiose?

Turning to another medium, but to a mind no less original, here's an excerpt from *Living-Room War* by Michael J.
Arlen. The book is a collection of the critical columns on
television that Arlen wrote for *The New Yorker* during
1966–67.

Vietnam is often referred to as "television's war," in
the sense that this is the first war that has been brought
to the people preponderantly by television. People indeed look at television. They really look at it. They look
at Dick Van Dyke and become his friend. They look at
thoughtful Chet Huntley and find him thoughtful, and
at witty David Brinkley and find him witty. They look at
Vietnam. They look at Vietnam, it seems, as a child
kneeling in the corridor, his eye to the keyhole, looks at
two grownups arguing in a locked room—the aperture
of the keyhole small; the figures shadowy, mostly out of
sight; the voices indistinct, isolated threats without
meaning; isolated glimpses, part of an elbow, a man's
jacket (who is the man?), part of a face, a woman's face.
Ah, she is crying. One sees the tears. (The voices con-

tinue indistinctly.) One counts the tears. Two tears. Three tears. Two bombing raids. Four seek-and-destroy missions. Six administration pronouncements. Such a fine-looking woman. One searches in vain for the other grownup, but, ah, the keyhole is so small, he is somehow never in the line of sight. Look! There is General Ky. Look! There are some planes returning safely to the *Ticonderoga*. I wonder (sometimes) what it is that the people who run television think about the war, because *they* have given us this keyhole view; we have given them the airwaves, and now, at this crucial time, they have given back to us this keyhole view—and I wonder if they truly think that those isolated glimpses of elbow, face, a swirl of dress (who *is* that other person anyway?) are all that we children can stand to see of what is going on inside the room.

This is criticism at its best: stylish, allusive, disturbing. It disturbs us—as criticism often should—because it jogs a firmly held set of beliefs and forces us to re-examine them. What holds our attention here is the metaphor of the keyhole, so exact and yet so mysterious. But what remains is a fundamental question about how a country's most powerful medium was telling the country's people about the war that they were fighting—and escalating. The column ran in 1966, when most Americans still supported the Vietnam war. Would they have turned against it sooner if TV had widened the keyhole, had shown us not only the "swirl of dress" but the severed head and the burning child? It's too late now to know. But at least one critic was keeping watch. Critics should always be among the first to notify us when the truths we hold to be self-evident cease to be true.

Some arts, of course, are harder to catch in print than others. One is dance, which consists of movement. How can a writer freeze all the graceful leaps and pirouettes? Another

is music. It's an art that we receive through our ears, yet the
writer is stuck with describing it in words that we will see.
At best he can only partly succeed, and many a music critic
has built a long career by hiding from his readers behind a
hedge of Italian technical terms. He will find just a shade too
much *rubato* in a pianist, a tinge of shrillness in a soprano's
tessitura.

But even in this world of evanescent notes a good critic
can make sense of what happened by writing good English
and by using references that mere mortals can understand.
Virgil Thomson, whose columns ran in the *New York Herald
Tribune* from 1940 to 1954, was an elegant practitioner. A
composer himself, an erudite and cultivated man, he still
never forgot that his readers were real people, and he wrote
with a zest that swept them along, his style alive with pleasant surprises. He also never forgot that musicians are real
people, and he didn't hesitate to shrink the giants to human
scale. What other critic would dare to secularize the sainted
Toscanini?

> It is extraordinary how little musicians discuss among
> themselves Toscanini's rightness or wrongness about
> matters of speed and rhythm and the tonal amenities.
> Like other musicians, he is frequently apt about these
> and as frequently in error. What seems to be more im-
> portant is his unvarying ability to put over a piece. He
> quite shamelessly whips up the tempo and sacrifices
> clarity and ignores a basic rhythm, just making the mu-
> sic, like his baton, go round and round, if he finds his
> audience's attention tending to waver. No piece has to
> mean anything specific; every piece has to provoke from
> its hearers a spontaneous vote of acceptance. This is
> what I call the "wow technique."

No *rubatos* or *tessituras* there, and no blind hero-worship.
Yet the paragraph catches the essence of what made

Toscanini great—an extra helping of showbiz. If his wor-
shipers are offended to think that the essence contained so
coarse an ingredient, they can continue to admire the
Maestro for his "lyrical colorations" or "orchestral *tuttis*." I'll
go along with Thomson's diagnosis, and so, I suspect, would
the Maestro.

Here, on the other hand, is Thomson analyzing pure mu-
sicianship, telling us why a piano recital by Josef Lhevinne
was not only perfect in itself but significantly better than the
work of other major artists:

> Any authoritative execution derives as much of its ex-
> cellence from what the artist does not do as from what
> he does. If he doesn't do anything off color at all, he is
> correctly said to have taste. Mr. Lhevinne's taste is as
> authoritative as his technical method. Not one sectarian
> interpretation, not one personal fancy, not one stroke
> below the belt, not a sliver of ham, mars the universal
> acceptability of his readings. Everything he does is right
> and clear and complete. Everything he doesn't do is the
> whole list of all the things that mar the musical execu-
> tions of lesser men.

Today, in his late eighties, Thomson is still at it, writing
with undiminished verve. Here's a recent article called "On
Writing Operas and Staging Them":

> Let me begin by talking about feeling at home in the-
> aters, having stage sense. It means an awareness of the
> fact that in show business—any kind of it—there is a
> show and there is an audience. It takes two to play the-
> ater.
> Historically speaking, not all the great poets, nor mu-
> sicians either, have been gifted for the stage. Shake-
> speare, Ben Jonson, Marlowe, Ford and Dryden all
> were. Milton was not. Nor were the great Romantics—

Byron, Shelley, Keats and Coleridge. Any more than
were the novelists and storytellers, from Sterne through
Dickens and on to Henry James, Proust and Joyce.

George Friedrich Handel was thoroughly a stage
man. Johann Sebastian Bach was not, though his *Saint
Matthew Passion*, with its moving recitatives for Jesus,
its terrifying crowd scenes and its audience-participation
hymns, approaches the dramatic oratorio. Mozart had
an enormous stage gift; Haydn a very small one in spite
of his 15 operas; Beethoven almost none, though he as-
pired to it. But Weber was wise in the theater, and
Wagner virtually infallible.

What is this mysterious talent that seems to have
skipped half the population? It shows up in children as
impersonation, or as simply showing off, in the manip-
ulation of family and friends through charm, later as an
exploitation of adolescent sex appeal. Wherever the
stage sense is true, it is accompanied by an instinct for
timing. In playing comedy, as in telling a joke, timing is
almost the whole trick. Tragedy, sob stories and soap
opera require a less wary trajectory. Just keep them
going, tears will eventually flow.

In just four paragraphs Thomson has given us a grab bag of
oddities about the artistic temperament and has anchored his
point in a mystery that has puzzled all of us since the sand-
box: why some kids (usually not us) have a theatrical bent
and others don't. We willingly follow him on a flight that
touches down in many cultures as he surveys the problems
of giving birth to an opera that will live and breathe. And he
doesn't just tell us about composers and librettists. To him
all the arts are one, and he also turns his thoughts to poets
and choreographers and writers, reminding us, for instance,
that "no American playwright, not Tennessee Williams nor
Thornton Wilder nor Edward Albee nor even Eugene

O'Neill, has produced anything comparable in power to Melville's *Moby Dick* or to the novels of Hawthorne, . . . Theodore Dreiser, John Dos Passos and William Faulkner." The playful notion that our novelists have more dramatic sense than our playwrights is only one of many that Thomson sends us away with. We're delighted to have been along on the ride.

How should a good piece of criticism start? Again, you must orient the reader to the specialized world he is about to enter. Even if he is a broadly educated person he needs to be told or reminded of certain facts. You can't just throw him in the water and expect him to swim easily. The water has to be warmed up.

Notice how the following review of *Virginia Woolf*, a biography by Quentin Bell—from the *New York Times Book Review*—begins by summarizing the main details that we should know about Mrs. Woolf, about her paradoxical position in the world of letters, about her biographer and about her girlhood. Not until we possess this general information are we ready or interested enough to follow the critic, Michael Rosenthal, down more specific and scholarly paths.

Generally regarded as a genius by those who knew her, Virginia Woolf has long suffered from both the uncritical adulation and the virulent antipathy that genius frequently inspires. Lost in the conflict between those who worship at the altar of her sensitivity and those who decry her as snobbish, desiccated and irrelevant is any substantial notion of who Virginia Woolf actually was. Quentin Bell brings an impressive set of intellectual and genetic credentials to the task of unraveling the enigma of the "high priestess of Bloomsbury." As the son of Clive and Vanessa Bell and the nephew of Virginia, Bell would seem to be the most qualified person to reveal the facts of her life. An art critic of as much substance

but less influence than his father, he has previously
written a slim volume evaluating the Bloomsbury circle
in which he grew up, and it was no surprise that
Leonard Woolf, Virginia's husband, should have encouraged Bell to undertake the authorized biography.
The results are in many ways startling.

The stage is well set. The final word, "startling," compels us
to go on. How is the book startling?

Born in 1882, Virginia was the third of four children
that Julia Duckworth Stephen, a young widow with
three children of her own, presented Sir Leslie Stephen, the eminent Victorian whose sober rationalism
and incessant self-pitying are immortalized in Mr. Ram-
say of *To the Lighthouse*. The Stephen household was in
fact very much like the Ramsays'; nourished by the
warmth and compassion of their mother, the seven children regarded the austere Sir Leslie with proper Victorian respect. But although there were certain
emotional disadvantages in having for a father the man
who in addition to editing the monumental *Dictionary
of National Biography* managed to produce 15 assorted
volumes of history, biography and criticism and well
over 100 long articles, there were a number of benefits
as well. Virginia grew up in an atmosphere densely
packed with words, ideas and, above all, books. . . .

It sounds normal enough—a respectable upper-middle-
class Victorian brood "clothed in the mantle of propriety," as
the critic puts it. "But no future study of Virginia Woolf will
ever be able to look at her life in quite the same way," he
continues, and we are off into the unwrapping of layers of
lurking madness and sexual experimentation, without which,
it now seems, no respectable upper-middle-class Victorian
family was complete. By the end of the review we see how

the author's public art and private suffering were intertwined from her childhood on, and why suicide was the inevitable end of both. But we had to begin with a plain set of facts.

Today criticism has many first cousins in journalism: the newspaper or magazine column, the essay, the editorial, and the essay-review, in which a critic digresses from a particular book or cultural phenomenon into a larger point. (Gore Vidal, for instance, has brought a high impudence to the form.) Many of the same principles that govern good criticism go into these columns. A political columnist, for instance, must love politics and know its ancient, tangled threads.

But what is common to all the forms is that they consist of personal opinion. Even the editorial that uses "we" was obviously written by an "I." And what is crucial for you as the writer is to express your opinion firmly. Don't cancel its strength with last-minute evasions and escapes. The most boring sentence in the daily newspaper is the last sentence of the editorial, which says that "it is still too early to tell whether the new policy will work" or that "the effectiveness of the decision remains to be seen." If it's still too early to tell, don't bother us with it at all, and as for what remains to be seen, *everything* remains to be seen, including what you'll be doing ten minutes from now. Take your stand with conviction.

Many years ago when I was writing editorials for the *New York Herald Tribune*, the editor of the page was a huge and ungainly man from Texas. I respected him because he had no pretense and because he hated any undue circling around a subject. Every morning we would all discuss what editorials we would like to write for the next day and what position we would take. Frequently we weren't quite sure, especially the writer who was an expert on Latin America.

"What about that coup in Uruguay?" the editor would ask.

"It could represent progress for the economy," the writer would reply, "or then again it might destabilize the whole political situation. I suppose I could mention the possible benefits and then . . ."

"Well," the man from Texas would break in, "let's not go peeing down both legs."

It was a plea that he made often, and it was perhaps the most inelegant advice I ever received. But over a long career of writing reviews and columns and trying to make a point that I felt strongly about, it was also probably the best.

19. Humor

Humor is the secret weapon of the nonfiction writer. It's secret because so few writers realize that it is often their best tool—and sometimes their only tool—for making an important point.

If this strikes you as a paradox, you're not alone. The professional writer of humor lives with the knowledge that half of his readers never know what he is trying to do. I remember a reporter calling to ask how I happened to write a certain parody in *Life*. At the end he said, "Should I refer to you as a humorist? Or have you also written anything serious?"

The answer, of course, is that if you're trying to write humor, almost everything you do is serious. Few Americans understand this. We dismiss our humorists as triflers because they have never settled down to "real" work. So the Pulitzer Prizes go to authors like Ernest Hemingway and William Faulkner, who are (God knows) serious and are therefore certified as men of literature. The prize has never gone to people like George Ade, H. L. Mencken, Ring Lardner, Robert Benchley, S. J. Perelman, Art Buchwald, Jules Feiffer and Woody Allen, who seem to be just fooling around.

They're not just fooling around. They are as serious in purpose as Hemingway or Faulkner—in fact, a national asset in forcing the country to see itself clearly. To them humor is urgent work. It's an attempt to say important things in a special way that regular writers aren't getting said in a regular way—or, if they are, it's so regular that nobody is reading it.

One cartoon by Herblock or Bill Mauldin is worth a hundred solemn editorials. One *Doonesbury* comic strip by Garry Trudeau—on the tendency of voters to re-elect convicted congressmen, or the tendency of Reagan's environmental agency to not protect the environment—is worth a thousand words of moralizing. One *Catch-22* or *Dr. Strangelove* is more powerful than all the books and movies that try to show war "as it is." They are two works of comic imagination, but they are still the standard points of reference for anyone trying to warn us about the military mentality that could blow us all up tomorrow. Joseph Heller and Stanley Kubrick heightened the truth about war just enough to catch its essential lunacy, and we recognize it as lunacy. The joke is no joke.

This heightening of some crazy truth—to a level where it will be seen as crazy—is at the heart of what the serious humorist is trying to do. I'll give you an example that may help to explain how he goes about his mysterious work.

One day in the 1960s I realized that half the girls and women in America were suddenly wearing haircurlers. It was of course an incredible new blight, and it was puzzling because I couldn't imagine when the girls took the curlers out. There was no evidence that they ever did. They wore them to the supermarket and to church and on dates, and quite possibly to their own weddings, and to many other places where they would be seen by many people. So what was the wonderful event they were saving the wonderful hairdo for?

I tried for a year to think of a way to write about this phenomenon. I could have come right out and said "It's an outrage," "It's a national disgrace" and "Have these women no pride?" But that would have been a sermon, and sermons are the death of humor. The writer must find some comic device—satire, parody, irony, lampoon, nonsense—that he can use to disguise his serious point. Very often he never finds it, because it's hard to find, and the point doesn't get made.

Luckily, my vigil was at last rewarded. I was browsing at my local newsstand and saw four magazines side by side: *Hairdo, Celebrity Hairdo, Combout* and *Pouf*. I bought all four—to the alarm of my news dealer—and found that there's a whole thriving world of journalism devoted solely to hair: life from the neck up, but not including the brain. The magazines had hundreds of diagrams of elaborate roller positions, and they also had lengthy columns in which a girl could send her roller problem to the editors for their advice. This was what I had needed. I invented a magazine called *Haircurl* and wrote a series of parody letters and replies. The piece ran in *Life* and it began like this:

Dear Haircurl:

I am 15 and am considered pretty in my group. I wear baby pink rollers, jumbo size. I have been going steady with a certain boy for 2½ years and he has never seen me without my rollers. The other night I took them off and we had a terrible fight. "Your head looks small," he told me. He called me a dwarf and said I had misled him. How can I win him back?

HEARTSICK
Speonk, N.Y.

Dear Heartsick:

You have only yourself to blame for doing something so stupid. The latest "Haircurl" survey shows that 94% of American girls now wear rollers in their hair 21.6 hours a day and 359 days a year. You tried to be different and you lost your fella. Take our advice and get some super-jumbo rollers (they come in your favorite baby pink shade, too) and your head will look bigger than ever and twice as lovely. Don't ever take them off again.

Dear Haircurl:

My problem is an intimate one, but I'm so upset that I just have to ask your advice. My boyfriend likes to run his fingers through my hair. The trouble is he keeps getting them pinched in my rollers. The other night a terribly embarrassing episode happened. We were at the movies and somehow my boyfriend got two of his fingers caught (it was right where the medium roller meets the clip-curl) and couldn't get them out. I felt very conspicuous leaving the theater with his hand still in my hair, and going home on the bus several people gave us "funny looks." Fortunately I was able to reach my stylist at home and he came right over with his tools and got poor Jerry loose. Jerry was very mad and said he's not going to date me again until I get some rollers that don't have this particular habit. I think he is being unfair, but he "means business." Can you help me?

FRANTIC
Buffalo

Dear Frantic Buffalo:

We're sorry to have to tell you that no rollers have yet been developed that do not occasionally catch the fingers of boys who tousle. The roller industry, however, is working very hard on the problem, as this complaint frequently comes up. Meanwhile why not ask Jerry to wear mittens? That way you'll be happy and he'll be safe.

There were many more, and perhaps the article even made a small contribution to Lady Bird Johnson's "beautification" program. But the point is this: once you've read that article you can never look at haircurlers again in quite the same way. You've been jolted by humor into looking with a fresh eye at something bizarre in our daily environment that was previously taken for granted. This is what the serious humorist is trying to do. The subject here isn't important— haircurlers certainly won't be the ruin of our society. But the method will work for subjects that *are* important, or for almost any subject, if you can find the right comic frame.

Over the last five years of the old *Life*, 1968–1972, I used humor to get at all kinds of subjects that might seem highly improbable. Quite a few columns were on the excesses of military power and procurement and on nuclear testing and radioactive leaks. One was on the petty squabbling over the shape of the table at the Vietnam peace conference in Paris. The situation had become so outrageous after nine weeks that it could only be approached through high ridicule, and I described various efforts to get peace at my own dinner table by changing its shape every night, or by lowering the chairs of different people to give them less "status," or by turning their chairs around so that the rest of us wouldn't have to "recognize" them. It was absurd, but no more absurd than what was happening in Paris.

What made the pieces work as parody was that they stuck close to the form they were parodying. Humor may seem to be an act of gross exaggeration. But the haircurler letters wouldn't succeed if we didn't recognize them as a specific journalistic form, both in their style and in their mentality. Control is vital to humor. Don't use comical names like "Throckmorton." Don't repeat the same kind of joke two or three times—the reader will enjoy himself more if you only make it once. Trust the sophistication of readers who *do* know what you're doing, and don't worry about the rest.

The columns that I wrote for *Life* made people laugh. But they all had a serious purpose, which was to say: "Something grotesque is going on here—some erosion in the quality of life, or some threat to life itself, and yet everyone assumes that it's normal." Today in America the outlandish becomes routine overnight. The humorist is trying to say that it really is still outlandish.

I remember a cartoon by Bill Mauldin during the student turmoil of the late 1960s, when infantrymen and tanks were summoned to keep peace at a college in North Carolina and undergraduates at Berkeley were dispersed by a helicopter spraying them with Mace. The cartoon showed a mother pleading with her son's draft board: "He's an only child— please get him off the campus." It was Mauldin's way of pinning down this particular lunacy, and he was right on target. In fact, he was at the center of the bull's-eye, as Kent State and Jackson State proved not long after his cartoon appeared.

Obviously the targets will change from week to week and from year to year. But there will never be a dearth of new lunacies—and dangers—for the humorist to detect and to fight. Lyndon Johnson in the years of his Vietnamization was brought down partly by Jules Feiffer and Art Buchwald. Joseph McCarthy and Spiro Agnew were brought down partly by Walt Kelly in the comic strip *Pogo*. H. L. Mencken brought down a whole galaxy of hypocrites in high places, and "Boss" Tweed was partly toppled by the cartoons of Thomas Nast.

Mort Sahl, a comic, was the only person who stayed awake during the Eisenhower years, when all of America was under sedation and didn't want to be roused. Many people regarded Sahl as a cynic, but he thought of himself as an idealist. "If I criticize somebody," he said, "it's because I have higher hopes for the world, something good to replace the bad. I'm not saying what the Beat Generation says: 'Go away because I'm not involved.' I'm here and I'm involved."

"I'm here and I'm involved"—make this your creed if you seriously want to write serious humor. The humorist operates on a deeper current than most people suspect. He must not only make a strong point; he must be willing to go against the grain, to state what the populace and the Presi-

dents may not want to hear. Art Buchwald and Garry Trudeau perform an act of courage at least once a week. They
say things that need to be said but that a regular columnist
couldn't get away with. What saves them is that politicians
are not known for humor and are therefore even more be-
fuddled by it than the citizenry.

It's a lonely and perilous calling. No other kind of writer
risks his neck so visibly on the high wire of public approval,
and the humorist knows that he will frequently fall off. Yet
he is in dead earnest, this acrobat bobbing over our heads,
trying to startle us with nonsense into seeing our lives with
sense.

But of course humor has many uses besides the merely
topical. They aren't as urgent because they don't address
problems of the day. But they are equally important because
they help us to look at far older problems of the heart, the
home, the job and all the other frustrations of just getting
from morning to night.

In 1970 I interviewed the late Chic Young, creator of
Blondie, when he had been writing and drawing that strip—
daily and Sunday—for forty years, or 14,500 strips. It was
the most popular of all comic strips, reaching 60 million
readers in every corner of the world and in many languages,
and I asked him the secret of its durability.

"It's durable because it's simple," he said. "It's built on
four things that everybody does: sleeping, eating, raising a
family and making money." The comic twists on these four
themes are as various in the strip as they are in life. Dagwood's efforts to get money from his boss, Mr. Dithers, have
their perpetual counterweight in Blondie's efforts to spend
it. "I try to keep Dagwood in a world that people are used
to," Young said. "He never does anything as special as playing golf, and the people who come to the door are just the
people that an average family has to deal with."

I cite Young's four themes as a reminder that most humor,
however freakish it may seem, is based on fundamental

truths. Humor is not a separate organism that can survive on its own frail metabolism. It's a special angle of vision granted to certain writers who already write good English. They are not writing about life that's essentially ludicrous. They are writing about life that's essentially serious, but their vision focuses on the areas where serious hopes are mocked by some ironic turn of fate—"the strange incongruity," as Stephen Leacock put it, "between our aspiration and our achievement."

E. B. White also emphasizes that the humor writer is not some sort of maverick unrelated to the rest of the herd. "I don't like the word 'humorist,'" he says. "It seems to me misleading. Humor is a by-product that occurs in the serious work of some and not others. I was more influenced by Don Marquis than by Ernest Hemingway, by Perelman than by Dreiser."

Therefore I would suggest several principles for the writer of humor. Master the craft of writing good "straight" English; humorists from Mark Twain to Russell Baker are, first of all, superb writers. Don't search high and low for the outlandish and scorn what seems too ordinary; you will touch more chords by finding what is funny in what you know to be true. Finally, don't strain for laughs; humor is built on surprise, and you can surprise the reader only so often.

Unfortunately for the writer, humor is elusive and subjective. No two people think the same things are funny, and an article that one magazine will reject as a dud is often published by another that finds it hilarious. The reasons for rejection are also elusive. "It just doesn't work," editors say, and there's not much that they can add. Occasionally such a piece can be made to work—it has some flaw that can be repaired. Mortality, however, is high, and diagnosis generally futile. "Humor can be dissected, as a frog can," E. B. White once wrote, "but the thing dies in the process and the innards are discouraging to any but the pure scientific mind."

I'm no fancier of dead frogs, but I wanted to see if at least a few lessons could be learned by poking about in the innards, and one year when I was at Yale I decided to teach a course in humor writing. I warned my students that I didn't think it had ever been tried, that quite possibly it couldn't be done, and that we might end up killing the thing we loved. Luckily, humor not only didn't die; it bloomed in the encircling desert of solemn term papers, and I subsequently taught the course again. Let me try briefly to reconstruct our journey.

"I hope to point out that American humor has an honorable literature," I wrote in a memo for prospective students, "and to consider the influence of certain pioneers on their successors. . . . Though the line between 'fiction' and 'nonfiction' is often fuzzy in humor, I see this as a nonfiction course—what you write will be based on external events. I am not interested in 'creative writing,' flights of pure imagination, and pointless whimsy."

I began by reading brief excerpts from early writers to show that a humorist can use a wide range of literary forms, or invent new ones. We started with George Ade's "Fables in Slang," the first of which appeared in 1897 in the *Chicago Record*, where Ade was a reporter. "He was just sitting unsuspectingly in front of a sheet of paper," Jean Shepherd writes in a fine introduction to his anthology, *The America of George Ade*, "when the innocent idea came to him to write something in fable form using the language and the clichés of the moment. In other words, slang. He said that to let people know that he knew better than to use slang in writing, he decided to capitalize all suspicious words and phrases. He was mortally afraid people would think he was illiterate."

He needn't have worried; by 1900 the Fables were so popular that he was earning $1,000 a week. Here, for instance, is "The Fable of the Subordinate Who Saw a Great Light":

Once there was an Employé who was getting the Nub

End of the Deal. He kicked on the long Hours and the small Salary, and helped to organize a Clerks' Protective Association. He was for the Toiler as against the Main Squeeze.

To keep him simmered down, the Owners gave him an Interest. After that he began to perspire when he looked at the Pay-Roll, and it did seem to him that a lot of big, lazy Lummixes were standing around the shop doing the Soldier Act. He learned to snap his Fingers every time the Office Boy giggled. As for the faithful old Book-Keeper who wanted an increase to $9 and a week's Vacation in the Summer, the best he got was a little Talk about Contentment being a Jewel.

The saddest moment of the Day for him was when the whole Bunch knocked off at 6 o'clock in the Evening. It seemed a Shame to call 10 Hours a Full Day. As for the Saturday Half-Holiday Movement, that was little better than Highway Robbery. Those who formerly slaved alongside of him in the Galleys had to address him as Mister, and he had them numbered the same as Convicts.

One Day an Underling ventured to remind the Slave-Driver that once he had been the Friend of the Salaried Minion.

"Right you are," said the Boss. "But when I plugged for the lowly Wage-Earner I never had been in the Directors' Office to see the beautiful Tableau entitled 'Virtue copping out the Annual Dividend.' I don't know that I can make the situation clear to you, so I will merely remark that all those who get on our side of the Fence are enabled to catch a new Angle on this Salary Question."

Moral: *For Educational Purposes, every Employé should be taken into the Firm.*

The universal truth in that brief gem is still true ninety

years later, as it is in almost all the Fables. "Ade was my first
influence as a humorist," Perelman once said. "He had a social sense of history. His pictures of Hoosier life at the turn
of the century are more documentary than any of those studies on how much people paid for their coal. His humor was
rooted in a perception of people and places. He had a cutting edge and an acerbic wit that no earlier American humorist had."

Next I dipped into Ring Lardner, partly to demonstrate
that dramatic dialogue, or the playlet, is another form that
can serve the humorist. I'm a pushover for Lardner's nonsense plays, which he must have written just to amuse himself. But I suspect that he was also lampooning the holy
conventions of playwriting, in which yards of italic type are
used presumably to explain what's happening on stage. I
share Lardner's obvious doubt that these stage directions are
meant for anyone to read or to fathom.

My favorite Lardner play, *I Gaspiri (The Upholsterers)*,
begins with the usual list of "Characters." I mean it's the
usual list; they are not the usual characters:

Ian Obri, *a Blotter Salesman*
Johan Wasper, *his wife*
Greta, *their daughter*
Herbert Swope, *a nonentity*
Ffena, *their daughter, later their wife*
Egso, *a Pencil Guster*
Tono, *a Typical Wastebasket*

Act I consists of ten lines of dialogue, none of it involving
these characters, and nine lines of irrelevant italic, con-
cluding with: "The curtain is lowered for seven days to de-
note the lapse of a week." This leads into Act III, which, we
are told, takes place on the Lincoln Highway with "two
bearded glue lifters seated at one side of the road." This is
followed by a long italic translator's note explaining the prin-

cipal industry in Phlace, which is hoarding hay, whereupon
the play concludes:

> FIRST GLUE LIFTER: Well, my man, how goes it?
> SECOND GLUE LIFTER: *(Sings "My Man," to show
> how it goes.)*

We savored this for the pleasure of nonsense as a humor
form in itself, often masking some deeper annoyance on the
part of the writer. Then I resurrected *Archy and Mehitabel,*
by Don Marquis, to show that this influential humorist also
used an unlikely medium—doggerel—for his message. Marquis, a columnist for the *New York Sun,* stumbled on a novel
solution to the newspaperman's brutal problem of meeting a
deadline and presenting his material in an orderly form, just
as Ade stumbled on the fable. In 1916 he created the cock-
roach Archy, who banged out free verse on Marquis' typewriter at night, minus capital letters because he wasn't
strong enough to press the shift key.

Archy's poems, describing his friendship with a cat named
Mehitabel, are of a philosophical bent that one wouldn't
guess from their ragged appearance. No formal essay, for instance, could more thoroughly deflate all the aging actors
who bemoan the current state of the theater than Marquis
does in "The Old Trouper," a long poem in which Archy
describes Mehitabel's meeting with an old theater cat named
Tom:

> i come of a long line
> of theatre cats
> my grandfather
> was with forrest
> he had it he was a real trouper
> my grandfather said
> he had a voice
> that used to shake
> the ferryboats

on the north river
once he lost his beard
and my grandfather
dropped from the
fly gallery and landed
under his chin
and played his beard
for the rest of the act
you don t see any theatre
cats that could do that
nowadays
they haven t got it they
haven t got it
here . . .

Marquis uses humor to leaven his impatience with a type of bore he knew well. It is of course a universal impatience, whatever the category of old-timer, just as it's a universal trait of old-timers to complain that their profession has gone to the dogs. Marquis achieves one of the classic functions of humor: to deflect anger into a channel where we can laugh at frailty instead of railing against it.

To illustrate parody I chose some passages from Thurber's nudge at Fowler's *Modern English Usage,* a book which, for all its eminence, can get (as Fowler would never allow me to say) mighty tiresome. Thurber has expressed with parody what I have often felt myself. Like Marquis, he has provided the humorist's gift of catharsis:

The number of people who use "whom" and "who" wrongly is appalling. Take the common expression, "Whom are you, anyways?" That is of course, strictly speaking, correct—and yet how formal, how stilted! The usage to be preferred in ordinary speech and writing is "Who are you, anyways?" "Whom" should be used in the nominative case only when a note of dignity or austerity is desired. For example, if a writer is dealing with a meeting of, say, the British Cabinet, it would be better to have the Premier greet a new arrival, such as an under-secretary, with a "Whom are you, anyways?" rather than a "Who are you, anyways?"—always granted that the Premier is sincerely unaware of the man's identity. To address a person one knows by a "Whom are you?" is a mark either of incredible lapse of memory or inexcusable arrogance.

The next writers on my tour were Donald Ogden Stewart and Robert Benchley, two men who greatly broadened for their successors the possibilities of "free-association" humor, opening whole new territory. Typical of Stewart's reckless bravery—for the 1920s—is the opening of his book *The Crazy Fool:*

This is a story about a crazy fool named Charlie Hatch who inherited an insane asylum from his uncle. When he inherited the asylum, Charlie was 23 years old and in love, which made his total age 14 including depreciation and money for carfare and marbles.

Benchley was just as crazy a fool and perhaps even more daring, for he wrote in his own voice, adding a dimension of warmth and vulnerability that was not present in humorists like Ade and Marquis, who ducked into other forms such as fable and doggerel. Nobody has ever been better than Benchley at diving headlong into his subject:

I have always tried to be as public-spirited as I could and yet save out a little time to myself for running and jumping. When the Fuel Administration wanted us all to save coal, I saved coal with a will; when it was Anti-Litter Week, I anti-littered; when the nation was supposed to be devoting itself to eating apples, I drank applejack until the cows came home—and very funny-looking cows they were, too.

St. Francis of Assisi (unless I am getting him mixed up with St. Simeon Stylites, which might be very easy to do as both their names begin with "St.") was very fond of birds, and often had his picture taken with them sitting on his shoulders and pecking at his wrists. That was all right, if St. Francis liked it. We all have our likes and dislikes, and I have more of a feeling for dogs.

Perhaps they were all just paving the way for Perelman. In any case, Perelman gratefully acknowledged these debts. "You must learn by imitation," he said. "I could have been arrested for imitating Lardner in my pieces in *Judge* in the late 1920s—not the content, but the manner. These influences gradually fall away."

His own influence, however, has not been so easily shed. At his death in 1979 he had been writing steadily for more than half a century, putting the language through some of its most breathtaking loops, and in both America and England the woods are still full of writers and comics who were drawn into the gravitational pull of Perelman's style and never quite got back out. It doesn't take a detective to see his hand not only in such brilliant modern writers as Woody Allen, but in the BBC's *Goon Show* and *Monty Python,* in the radio skits of Bob and Ray, and in the glancing wit of Groucho Marx—an influence more easily traceable because Perelman wrote several of the Marx Brothers' early movies.

What he created was an awareness that when the writer's mind works by free association it can ricochet from the normal to the absurd and, by the very unexpectedness of its angle, demolish whatever trite idea had been there before. To this element of perpetual surprise—after fifty years, Perelman's readers still never knew what was coming next—he grafted the dazzling wordplay that is his trademark, a vocabulary incredibly rich and recondite, and an erudition based on constant reading and travel. Still, even so rare a mixture wouldn't have sustained him if he hadn't always had a target.

"All humor must be *about* something—it must touch concretely on life," he said, and though readers in their pure enjoyment of his style may lose sight of his deeper motive, some form of pomposity usually lies in ruins at the end of a Perelman piece, just as grand opera never quite recovered from the Marx Brothers' *A Night at the Opera* or banking from W. C. Fields' *The Bank Dick*. In the 1930s, Perelman recalled, "advertisers were giving themselves the most colossal airs, bombinating away about the creative importance of what they were doing," and many of his early satires and parodies lanced the fatuous ad campaigns of that era. But he was never at a loss for charlatans and knaves, especially in the worlds of Broadway and Hollywood, merchandising, health, medicine, food, fashion, publishing and travel. He had a sure instinct for pretension and cupidity.

I still remember my exhilaration on first encountering Perelman's *New Yorker* pieces. They contained sentences unlike any that I had ever seen before, or even imagined, and they fractured me:

> The whistle shrilled and in a moment I was chugging out of Grand Central's dreaming spires. I had chugged only a few feet when I realized that I had left without the train, so I had to run back and wait for it to start. . . . With only two hours in Chicago I would be unable to see the city, and the thought drew me into a state of composure. I noted with pleasure that a fresh coat of grime had been given to the Dearborn Street station, though I was hardly vain enough to believe that it had anything to do with my visit.

> From the ostermoor where I was stretched out lazily, I murmured an inviting "Come in!"
> "Come in!" I murmured invitingly. He entered shaking himself vigorously. There had been a heavy fall of talcum several hours before and as far as the ground could see the eye was white.

Women loved this impetual Irish adventurer who would rather fight than eat and vice-versa. One night he was chafing at The Bit, a tavern in Portsmouth, when he overheard a chance remark from a brawny gunner's mate in his cups. . . . The following morning the "Maid of Hull," a frigate of the line mounting 36 guns, out of Bath and into bed in a twinkling, dropped downstream on the tide, bound for Bombay, object matrimony. On her as passenger went my great-grandfather. . . . Fifty-three days later, living almost entirely on cameo brooches and the ptarmigan which fell to the ptrigger of his pfowling piece, he at last sighted the towers of Ish-peming, the Holy City of the Surds and Cosines, fanatical Mohammedan warrior sects.

Obviously I could go on (and on), just as I could quote at length from all the writers I introduced to my class, ending with Woody Allen, certainly the most cerebral humorist around today. Allen's magazine pieces, collected in *Getting Even* and *Without Feathers*, constitute a body of written humor unique for being both intellectual and hilarious, probing not only his well-known themes of death and anxiety, but such overbearing academic disciplines and literary forms as philosophy, psychology, drama, Irish poetry and the explication of texts ("Hassidic Tales"). Nor is he buried solely in an interior world of scholarship and neurosis. "A Look at Organized Crime," a parody of all the articles ever written explaining the Mafia, is one of the funniest pieces I know, and "The Schmeed Memoirs"—the recollections of Hitler's barber—is the ultimate jab at the "good German" who was just doing his job:

I have been asked if I was aware of the moral implications of what I was doing. As I told the tribunal at Nuremberg, I did not know that Hitler was a Nazi. The truth was that for years I thought he worked for the phone company. When I finally did find out what a monster he was, it was too late to do anything, as I had made a down payment on some furniture. Once, toward the end of the war, I did contemplate loosening the Führer's neck-napkin and allowing some tiny hairs to get down his back, but at the last minute my nerve failed me.

None of the brief samplings in this chapter can convey more than a glimmer of the immense output and artistry of these writers. Nevertheless I wanted my students to know that they were operating within a long tradition of good writing and considerable nerve—a tradition that's still very much alive today, maintained by such bold and gifted humorists as Ian Frazier, Lynn Caraganis and Garrison Keillor.

I wanted my students to try their wings and to fly high. For the first weeks I told them to write in one of the existing humor forms—parody, lampoon, etc.—and not to use "I" or to write from personal experience. I assigned the same topic to the entire class, bringing in some current absurdity that I had noticed in the newspaper, in a magazine or in my mail. My best hopes were realized. What the students wrote was funny, inventive and often surrealistic. They jumped boldly into free association, nonsense and surprise. They learned that it was possible to throw off the chains of logic and to have fun making a serious point within a given humor form. They were heavily under the influence of Woody Allen's throwaway non sequiturs ("For this the Rabbi bashes his head in, which, according to the Torah, is one of the most subtle methods of showing concern").

After about four weeks, fatigue set in. The students had found that they were capable of writing humor. But they had also found how tiring it is to sustain a weekly act of comic invention, writing in other voices and formats. It was time to slow down their metabolism—to start them writing in their own voice and about their own experience. I declared a moratorium on reading Woody Allen and said I would tell them when they could read him again. That moment never came.

I adopted the Chic Young principle—stick to what you know—and began to read from writers who use humor as a vein that runs quietly through their work and leaves a cumulative pleasure. One piece was E. B. White's "The Eye of Edna," in which White recalls waiting on his Maine farm for the actual arrival of Hurricane Edna while listening for several days to inane radio reports of its progress. It's a perfect essay, full of wisdom and gentle wit. Another writer whose work I excavated was Stephen Leacock, a Canadian. I remembered him from my boyhood as hilarious, but was afraid that, as often happens in looking up old friends, he would turn out to be "comical" but not funny. On the contrary, his pieces had survived the erosion of time, and one that I particularly remembered—"My Financial Career," in which he tries to open a bank account with $56—still seems the model piece of humor on how rattled we all become when dealing with banks, libraries and other institutions. Rereading Leacock reminded me that still another function of the humorist is to represent himself as the victim or the dunce, helpless in most situations. This enables the reader to feel superior, or at least to identify with a fellow victim.

So that was the direction in which we began to move, the students trying—often with difficulty—to find their "voice" and to write about their own lives. Many of them wrote about their families. We ran into problems, mainly of exaggeration, and gradually solved them, trying to achieve control—cutting the extra sentence, for instance, which explains a funny point that is already implicit.

A hard decision was to know how much exaggeration was allowable and how much was too much. One student wrote a funny piece about what a terrible cook his grandmother was. When I praised it he said that she was really a very good cook. I said I was sorry to hear it—somehow the piece now seemed less funny. He asked if this made a difference. I said it didn't make a difference in this piece, since I had enjoyed it without knowing it was untrue, but that I thought he would last longer as a humorist if he started from the truth rather than from invention. In Thurber's story "The Night the Bed Fell," we know that he has slightly enlarged the facts; but we also know that *something* happened to the bed that night in the attic.

In short, our class began by striving first for humor and hoping to wing a few truths along the way. We ended by striving for truth and hoping to add humor along the way. Ultimately we realized that the two are intertwined.

Near the end of the term, Perelman came and talked to the class, giving us more to ponder, needless to say, than I can summarize here. But I'll leave the last word to him.

"When you endeavor to be funny in every line," he said, "you place an intolerable burden not only on yourself but on the reader. You have to allow the reader to breathe. Whenever George S. Kaufman saw three straight funny lines in a play that he was directing, he cut the first two. The fact is that all of us have only one personality, and we wring it out like a dish towel. I don't think you can constantly create a new identity if you're a comic writer. You are who you are."

PART **III**

Approaches

20. Writing—and Rewriting— with a Word Processor

There's nobody more filled with anxiety than a writer who has been told that he should start writing with a word processor. He keeps putting it off, and when he finally runs out of excuses he goes to his fate lugging more of the classic phobias than even Freud would want to see in one patient: fear of machines, fear of failure, fear of looking stupid, fear of writing, fear of separation from all that's familiar and comfortable.

And there's nobody more evangelistic than a writer who has made the leap. Like all evangelists, he has been given the good news, which is that a word processor not only frees writers from the drudgery of writing and rewriting and retyping; it also makes them better writers. Not since the typewriter replaced the pen has a more exciting tool come along. I don't know a single writer with a word processor who would dream of going back to the way he wrote before.

So the problem, obviously, is how to make the leap. How does the neurotic get turned into the believer? As a former neurotic I can testify that the first step is the hardest.

Like many writers, I'm a mechanical boob. I can't figure out how the simplest mechanism works. The stapler on my desk has been empty for a year. It's not that I haven't bought the staples; I just can't face the trauma of trying to put them in. One of the sights I most dread on the American landscape is a self-service gas station. I will drive back and forth through an entire town to find a station that has a human operator, one where I won't have to get out and stare at the pump handle, realizing—once again—that I have no idea how to release the gas. When I'm confronted by any strange contraption my hands shake and my heart begins to pound. Fear of flying, for instance, is not one of my phobias; what reduces me to panic in an airplane is trying to open those little plastic packets of food.

I mention this to explain that I'm a liberal arts type, with all the hang-ups that come out of that tradition—and also many of the snobberies. I'm as guilty as the next humanist of thinking that science and technology are what have made the world more cold and impersonal. I also come out of a tradition of dependence on paper. To me, paper and pencil were always holy objects. So were scissors and paste, and so were the floor and the wastebasket and all the other objects for arranging writing when it was going well and for throwing it away when it wasn't.

All my life I wrote by putting a piece of paper in an old Underwood standard typewriter. I would write one or two paragraphs, and then I would take the paper out and edit what I had written, and then I would put a new piece of paper in the typewriter and type what I had edited, and then I'd take *that* piece of paper out and edit it, and then I'd type it again. And again.

Nevertheless I began to see that a major revolution was under way in writing, editing, composition, layout, printing and publishing. Paper was out; type was out; Gutenberg was out. Electronic writing was in. Still, I tried to ignore it. Then, one day, my wife said, "You ought to write a book about how to write with a word processor." And she *knows* what a mechanical boob I am. But I thought: Why not? Instead of being dragged kicking and screaming into the future, I would drag everybody else kicking and screaming into the future.

So I went around to IBM. I'd like to say that I went the next day, but somehow I didn't. I chose IBM solely because it was one of the oldest and most respected companies in the field. I didn't want to waste time comparing brands. I also knew that if I didn't just go out and do it I would never do it at all.

At the showroom I was met by a young man and a young woman who showed me the IBM Displaywriter. They were impeccable in business suits. They sat me down among their gleaming terminals and I thought, "I'm not well enough dressed for the new technology. I'm a writer. God help me if I spill some Danish pastry on this stuff." The IBM woman, whose name was Donna, started to demonstrate the equipment. As she typed and pressed other mysterious keys, her words kept popping onto the screen and off again. Meanwhile she explained what she was doing in language that wasn't comforting: words like textpack and module and diskette. (A diskette is a disk; that's part of the problem.)

Then she said, "Now you try it." I said "I have to go." But Donna eased me over to the keyboard and told me to write something. "You're very tense," she said. I *was* tense. My hands were clammy; any minute I'd start hyperventilating all over their shiny equipment. I took off my coat and loosened my tie, and they were shocked by that, but at least I felt more like a writer. Still, I didn't think *my* words would appear on the screen; only IBM's words would appear on the screen.

But I started to type, and my words *did* appear on the screen. They even looked like my words. I had thought that writing at a terminal would involve whole new mental processes—that the machine would make my writing mechanical. But it seemed quite natural. I began to play with the keys that make it possible to insert new words and sentences, or to delete them or move them around, and I got the point, and I told Donna and Robert to sign me up. (The

IBM man's name was Robert; somehow I knew it wasn't
going to be Skip or Bud.) We signed the contract, incidentally, with a ballpoint pen on an old-fashioned form with car-
bon paper. When it's legal time at IBM they want you on
paper and not on a disk.

I arranged to have the word processor delivered to my
office at the Book-of-the-Month Club and I walked out into
the familiar streets of Manhattan and took a deep breath. I
had faced the unknown and come out alive. But I still had to
face the machine. As I waited for it to be delivered, I half
hoped it would never come. When it did, I managed for a
week to find reasons not to open the cartons, and when I
finally had assembled the five units—the keyboard, the terminal screen, the electronic module that the screen sits on,
the toaster-like unit that holds the disks, and the printer—I
waited another two days before I turned the power switch to
ON. That was the biggest step of all.

I taught myself to use the machine in about two weeks.
Today I realize that it's possible to teach a writer in one hour
almost everything he would need to know. But I was up
against three obstacles. One was that I was an early user of a
word processor; nobody else in our office had one, and there
was no friend to answer my questions. Another block was
that I was trying to learn from the instruction manual—one
of the most forbidding swamps in the English language.

But the biggest block was my basic fear of machines.
Every time my machine emitted a beep I jumped; every
time the screen wrote me one of its punitive messages, like
INVALID KEY or WRONG DISKETTE, I took it as a rebuke—I
was too dumb for the new technology. In fact, I kept feeling
guilty for making my word processor work so hard. I would
inadvertently make some sentences disappear, and then I
would have to ask the machine to get them back, and the
machine would retrieve them with a great deal of self-impor-
tant clunking and I would feel terrible about putting it to so

much trouble. Several weeks went by before I thought, "It's just a bunch of wires." This brilliant insight led to the first breakthrough: "I'm as smart as the machine."

The second breakthrough came when I realized that I didn't have to learn to do all the things the machine can do. The screen and the manuals constantly describe elaborate tasks that the word processor can perform: horrible tasks for secretaries who need to compile tables or indexes, for instance, or make blind copies of business correspondence. The breakthrough came when I thought: "I don't want to do all those tasks. I only want to write and rewrite and edit and paginate and print." At that moment the machine lost its power over me and I realized—the biggest breakthrough of all—that it's just a fancy typewriter.

What does a word processor do that's so helpful? It puts your words right in front of your eyes for your instant consideration—and reconsideration. Most writers don't initially say what they want to say, or say it as well as they could. The typical sentence as it first emerges almost always has something wrong with it: it's not clear; it's not logical; it's too long; it's full of clutter; it's awkward; it's pretentious; it's boring; it lacks rhythm; it could be read in several different ways; it doesn't lead the reader out of the previous sentence. As a writer you're well aware of this blunt truth and you know how to go back and make repairs. But you also know how tiring it is just to *think* about going back and making repairs. All of us have an emotional equity in our first draft—we can hardly believe that it wasn't born perfect. Beyond that, there's the fatigue of retyping the manuscript over and over. The tendency is to say, "It's good enough." Or you just run out of time.

But with a word processor you can play with your writing on the screen until you get it right, and the paragraphs will keep rearranging themselves, no matter how many words you change or add or cut, and you don't have to print it until it's just the way you want it. The printer will print exactly what's on the screen—word for word, line for line. It's an electronic typewriter that takes its instructions from the mother unit.

Imagine, for example, that you've written a paragraph. When you read it over you realize that there's something you'd like to add after the second sentence that hadn't occurred to you before. You just type it in. The existing sentences will move to the right to make room for it, and the paragraph will regroup itself with the new material added. Then let's say you read the new paragraph and find that you don't need the new sentence after all. Press the DELETE key. The sentence will vanish and the gaps will close up again. You can add or delete or move anything at all—words, phrases, sentences, paragraphs, whole pages. There's no kind of tinkering that you can't do—and undo—instantly.

To me this is God's gift, or technology's gift, to good writing. Because the essence of writing is rewriting. I've never thought of rewriting as an unfair burden—extra homework that I don't deserve. On the contrary, I think it's a privilege to be able to shape my writing until it's as clean and strong as I can make it. Like a good watch, it should run smoothly and have no extra parts. Nevertheless all this rewriting is a chore. I happen to be a slow writer, and I can't write the second paragraph until I've got the first one right, or the third one until I've got the second one right. The floor around my typewriter used to be littered with crumpled earlier drafts. I consoled myself with the truism that in the act of retyping, a writer is also rewriting. But now I see that the truism is only about 10 percent true: I've spent much of my life retyping, just as I spent a lot of time washing dishes by hand before someone invented the dishwasher. The word processor is the writer's dishwasher: it liberates you from a chore that's not creative and that saps your energy and enthusiasm.

Of course all writers write differently. My method of writing and rewriting one paragraph at a time is totally unlike that of the person who writes his whole first draft in one burst. Still, however you write, there's no escape from rewriting.

What do I mean by "rewriting"? I don't mean writing one version and then writing a whole new version from scratch, and then a third. Most rewriting consists of reshaping and polishing the raw material you wrote on your first try. This means that a certain amount of your typing has already been done. Let's look at a typical paragraph and imagine that it's the writer's first draft. There's nothing really wrong with it— it's clear and it's grammatical. But it's full of ragged edges: failures of the writer to keep the reader notified of changes in time, place and mood, or to animate his style. What I've done is to add, in brackets after each sentence, some of the thoughts that might occur to a careful writer taking a first look at this draft. After that the revised paragraph appears.

There used to be a time when neighbors took care of one another, he remembered. [*Put "he remembered" first to establish reflective tone.*] It no longer seemed to happen that way, however. [*The contrast supplied by "however" must start the sentence. Also establish place.*] He wondered if it was because everyone in the modern world was so busy. [*All these opening sentences are the same length and have the same dreary rhythm; turn this one around.*] It occurred to him that people today had so many things to do that they didn't have time any more for old-fashioned friendship. [*Sentence essentially repeats previous sentence; give it specific detail or kill it.*] Things didn't work that way in America in previous eras. [*Reader is still in the present tense; reverse the sentence to tell him he's now in the past. America no longer needed here if inserted earlier.*] And he knew that the situation was very different in other countries of the world, as he recalled from the years when he lived in villages in such places as Spain and Italy. [*Reader is still in America; start with a negative transition word. Sentence also too flabby. "Countries of the world" redundant.*] It almost seemed to him that as people got richer and built their houses farther apart they isolated themselves from the essentials of life. [*Plant irony early? Sharpen the paradox about richness.*] And there was another thought that troubled him. [*This is the real point of the paragraph; signal the reader that it's important. Avoid weak "there was" construction.*] His friends had deserted him when he needed them most during his recent illness. [*Reshape the sentence so the last word is "most"; the last word is the one that lingers in the reader's ear. Hold sickness for next sentence.*] It was almost as if they found him guilty of doing something shameful. [*Introduce sickness here as the reason. Is "guilty" necessary? Implicit?*] He recalled reading somewhere about societies in primitive parts of the world in which sick people were shunned, though he had never heard of any such ritual in America. [*Sentence starts slowly and stays very windy. Break it into shorter units. Snap off the point.*]

He remembered that neighbors used to take care of one another. But that no longer seemed to happen in America. Was it because everyone was so busy? Were people really so preoccupied with their TV sets and their cars and their fitness programs that they had no time for friendship? In previous eras that was never true. Nor was it how families lived in other parts of the world. Even in the poorest villages of Spain and Italy he recalled how people would drop in with a loaf of bread. An ironic idea struck him: as people got richer they cut themselves off from the richness of life. But what really troubled him was an even more shocking fact. The time when his friends deserted him was the time when he needed them most. By getting sick he almost seemed to have done something shameful. He knew that other societies had a custom of "shunning" people who were very ill. But that ritual only existed in primitive cultures. Or did it?

My revisions aren't necessarily the best ones that could be made—or the only ones. They're mainly matters of carpentry: fixing the structure and the flow. Much could still be done in such areas as cadence, detail and freshness of language. But my point is that most rewriting is a process of juggling elements that already exist. And I'm not just talking about polishing individual sentences. The total construction is equally important. Read your article aloud from beginning to end and put yourself in the reader's mind. You might find, for instance, that you had written two sentences like this:

> The tragic hero of the play is Othello. Small and malevolent, Iago feeds his jealous suspicions.

In itself there's nothing wrong with the Iago sentence. But as a sequel to the previous sentence it's very wrong. The name lingering in the reader's ear is Othello; as the reader proceeds into the next sentence he naturally assumes that Othello is small and malevolent.

When you read your writing aloud with these connecting links in mind you'll find a dismaying number of places where you have lost or confused the reader, or failed to tell him the one fact he needs to know, or told him too much. With a word processor you can move through your piece easily, patching all these trouble spots. After every patch, look at what you've done and decide whether you like it. If you don't, like it, try something else. When you finish your repairs the machine will paginate your entire article, putting the same number of lines on each page, and the printer will type it while you go and have a beer. Sweeter music could hardly be sung to a writer than the sound of his article being typed exactly the way he wants it—but not by him.

Later you may decide that you want to add a few paragraphs of new information on, say, page 8. Just call page 8 back to the screen, add the new material, and tell the machine to repaginate the article from that point forward. If you've forgotten a footnote—and what dissertation writer hasn't?—just type it in its proper place and let the machine do the dirty work of redistributing the lines, renumbering the pages and making a clean copy. Why should a Ph.D. candidate waste his intellect on such drudgery? His thesis is two years late anyway.

In short, the word processor can concentrate your mind on the craft of writing, revising and editing—much more powerfully than this has ever been possible, because your words are right in front of you in all their infinite possibility, waiting to be infinitely reshaped. Technology, the great villain, turns out to be your friend. I have no patience with people who say that writing at a terminal will make our writing mechanical, or turn our children into robots. What we write still has to come out of our heads; no machine is going to do that for us.

For children, in fact, the word processor strikes me as an ideal tool for learning how to write. Children are natural writers—their heads are full of images and wonder and wordplay. Their hands, however, are too slow to get all the wonderful words on paper. Grimly gripping the pencil, they try to keep pace with their galloping thoughts. But it's a losing battle—the joy of writing turns to frustration and is often lost forever. This wouldn't happen if they could tap out their writing easily and see it on a screen and move their words around and substitute one for another. *That's* the joy of writing, as every poet knows: to make words dance for us in all their possible patterns. The word processor could also be a classroom tool for teaching students how to revise and rewrite. Imagine that instead of a blackboard they would see a projection of a paragraph that's been written on a terminal screen, with the teacher editing the sentences and explaining his or her reasons. It would be a dramatic exposure to the writing process.

In my first few weeks at a word processor I was comforted by the thought that I could always make a printout of what I had written. Then I would be able to edit it with my sacred pencil. But very soon I realized that I was editing my writing on the screen more quickly and competently, and with far less fatigue, than I ever had on paper. Visually, the words seemed clearer when they were right in front of my eyes than when they were on a piece of paper viewed from a 45-degree angle. If even one letter was wrong it jumped out at me from the screen. And to be able to change those words instantly was a miracle. Every day I would just call up what I had written the day before, read over the last few pages and keep going. I only made a printout when somebody else needed a copy. I weaned myself from paper almost immediately.

But (I hear you saying) what if you decide after revising a paragraph that you liked the first version better? Especially that long opening sentence that caught the energy you were feeling at the time. And what was that elegant phrase—something about the gulls at dusk—that now seems so absolutely right, if not downright luminous? All those gems have vanished into the electricity. This question about the loss of material is the biggest factor—after the primordial fear of the machine itself—that keeps writers from even trying a word processor.

The question has various answers, depending on how you

work. In my case, editing and revising as I go along, I almost always prefer my improvements to what they replaced. I love to see an unnecessary word or phrase evaporate at the flick of a key; I love to replace a humdrum word with one that has more precision or color. With every change I feel that I'm getting nearer to where I would finally like to arrive, and as I see the piece growing in strength, literally before my eyes, I feel a purer pleasure than I've ever had in rewriting.

But most writers work in a more spacious manner, freely pouring out ideas and sentences with the knowledge that they can come back later and clean up the mess. If you are this kind of writer you don't want to keep erasing what you've written; you want to save all your drafts. You can do this on paper and you can also do it on the screen. The machine requires you to give a different name to every item you create at a terminal. This is the storage system that enables you to file your work on a disk and to summon it back as often as you need it.

Assume that you're writing an article about automobiles. You might name your first draft CAR. It will exist for you on a disk in that form, with all its raw virtues and flaws. You can also make a printout of it so that you have it on paper. Then you might write a second draft and name it CAR2 and make a printout of that. Then you might write a third draft, CAR3, by working from the printout of CAR and CAR2, combining the best features of both. Or you might decide that your well-meant revisions have lost the freshness of the original and that CAR is the version that's truest to your intentions. Just call CAR back to the screen and make it your working version, perhaps borrowing some refinements from CAR2 and CAR3. But whatever you do, the work will be much easier and faster because the words are only images of light.

In certain kinds of writing you'll save incredible amounts of time and energy. I'm thinking especially of interviews and other articles that make extensive use of "quotes." The people you interview may be highly articulate; nevertheless they will digress and repeat themselves. Even if they give you all the material you need, they will never give it to you in the form in which you'll finally need it. You're stuck with the hard job of imposing a shape on the material, distilling the quotes that will tell the story best, and creating a narrative flow.

This can involve hours of fiddling with the quotes: putting them in and taking them back out and trying them somewhere else and substituting different ones. Often, for instance, you'll write an entire page incorporating a set of quotes that you thought was perfect for a particular moment. Later you find in your notes a quote that makes the same point in a better way—it's more vivid, perhaps, or more exact. On a typewriter it would take twenty minutes to replace one quote with the other and retype the whole page. On a word processor you can do it painlessly in a minute or two.

Equally important are such matters as variety and pace. An article that just strings together long chunks of quotes, for instance, will soon become tiresome. You must periodically alter the rhythm by converting what the speaker said into a sentence of your own, explaining his point in your words. But often the only way to get a sense of the momentum of a piece is to write several paragraphs of quotes and then read them to see if they need to be broken up. Perhaps one brief sentence of yours can create a link more tightly than the speaker did.

What you must do, in short, is to make an arrangement— one that hangs together from beginning to end and that moves with economy and warmth. Such a structure can only be achieved with a fair amount of trial and error. And doing this on a screen certainly beats doing it over and over on a typewriter. My last book, *Willie and Dwike,* in which I was working mainly with oral material—information that people

had given me in their own words—took less than a year to
write on a word processor. On a typewriter it would have
taken at least two years. The difference was not only in
speed and morale; it was also in control. At the end I felt
that I had made exactly the arrangement that I had in mind
when I started.

These are crucial areas of gain for a writer: time, energy,
enthusiasm, output and control. I'm sure a word processor
would cut a year off the writing of a Ph.D. dissertation and
probably two. That's quite a bargain—in the business of
writing, time is money. For the dissertation writer, the
Ph.D. degree qualifies that person to enter the job market as
a professor. For the free-lance writer, every completed article liberates him or her to start the next one.

Nor is the saving limited to the writing; it also applies to
the publishing of what has been written. Normally when a
writer finishes a book manuscript the publisher allows six
months for it to be copyedited and typeset. In the case of
Willie and Dwike I gave a printout of my manuscript to
Harper & Row, where it was copyedited in a week. I made
the changes on my screen in a few hours and gave the publisher the two disks that contained my finished book. These
were converted directly into phototype and I had page
proofs three weeks later.

I learned a lot about myself by learning to write on a word
processor. I found that I could trust my powers of logic more
than I ever thought I could. When you realize that you're as
smart as the machine, you try to figure out how it has been
programmed to "think," and you find that you don't have to
be Einstein to think in the same sequential way. You say to
yourself, "If I want to do Z, the machine would probably
want me to do X and Y to get there," and you do it, and the
machine does it, and it's a wonderful moment. Somewhere
in the depths of your humanistic soul a little spark of satisfac-

tion goes off that you never knew was there. Logic turns out to be fun.

Which shouldn't be so surprising. The ability to think logically is one of the fundamental skills in nonfiction writing. Anyone who thinks logically should be able to write well; anyone whose thinking is fuzzy will never write well. I often think we should teach children simple logic before we teach them how to write.

I commend one thought to you as you dip your toe in the computer culture: You are more competent than you think you are. All of us liberal arts types have coddled ourselves with the notion that we can't perform mechanical tasks or understand technical processes. A lot of that is self-delusion—people will learn what they need to learn. In my case, as soon as I began to glimpse the countless ways in which a word processor could change my life I enjoyed thinking of all sorts of uses that would help me and my colleagues at work in our writing and our editing.

Still, resistance is strong. People listen to me and say, "I'm sure you're right—maybe next year I'll give it a try." They're afraid to give up the crutches they're sure they need to perform the act of writing. I knew, for instance, that I couldn't possibly write unless I could flick back and forth among several pieces of paper to see what I had written. I needed that continuity and I always would. Well, it turns out that I don't need it at all. On my screen I can see twenty lines at a time, and that's usually enough. If it isn't, I can bring the preceding lines into view. O.K., it's not ideal. But it's not fatal—the mind adjusts and develops new aptitudes.

The best way to take the plunge is to learn from another writer. Beginners assume that they have to take a computer course or immerse themselves in the instruction manual. But courses and manuals are meant mainly for office workers, who will use a word processor for office tasks. They are taught and written by people who aren't writers themselves and who don't know the cognitive steps that go into writing, revising and editing. By contrast, any writer who uses a word processor should be able to launch another writer in an hour. When I do this I demonstrate the relatively few functions that a writer needs, point out the keys that govern these functions and explain the logic that the machine uses to do what it does. Twenty minutes is generally enough. Then I sit my student down at the keyboard and tell him or her to write something. At first there is a timidity, as if to avoid striking a key that might blow the machine up. But this quickly dissolves into childlike pleasure. In fifteen minutes the beginner is writing paragraphs and adding and deleting words. All the fear is seen to have been unreasonable. At the end of an hour the worst is over.

Like most writers, I don't like to write; I like to have written. Now, however, I sit down to write far more willingly than I ever have before, especially if I'm facing a complex problem of organization. The opposite argument, of course, has also been made: because writing on a screen comes so easily and looks so neat it will make many people write worse; they will assume that their beautiful-looking words, so effortlessly born, are perfect. That's also true: sloppy writers may write even more sloppily. But a certain number of sloppy writers will improve, noticing for the first time the disarray of their thoughts on the screen and knowing that they have a second chance to make their sentences—and themselves—look better. Or a third chance. The machine is forgiving: it invites you to take risks, to try things out, to fly a little. If the flight doesn't work, nobody will ever know— you can delete it and try something else. But at least you have stretched your muscles and your sense of possibility. Maybe next time you will soar.

When you see your words on the screen, study them closely. Remember that the two cardinal virtues of writing are clarity and simplicity. Look for clutter and prune it out. Read your sentences aloud. Do they sound like you? If they don't, fiddle with them until they do. Don't say anything in writing that you wouldn't comfortably say in conversation. If you're not a person who says "indeed" or "moreover," or who calls someone an individual ("he's a fine individual"), don't ever write it. Are you drowning in long words? Think of shorter ones. Are your sentences full of abstract nouns like "productivity"? Turn the nouns into active verbs that get real people doing real things that the reader can picture. Is a sentence stiff and pompous? Relax and write a new one right after it that expresses the warm and lovable person you really are. Then delete the earlier sentence; the stiff and pompous you will vanish into the electricity. Use the machine, in short, to capture your humanity.

If that's a paradox, don't knock it.

21. Trust Your Material

The longer I work at the craft of writing, the more I realize that there's nothing more interesting than the truth. What people do—and what people say—continues to take me by surprise with its wonderfulness, or its quirkiness, or its drama, or its humor, or its pain. Who could invent all the astonishing things that really happen? Therefore I increasingly find myself saying to writers and students: "Trust your material."

Recently I spent some time as a writing coach at a newspaper in a small American city. I noticed that many of the reporters had fallen into the habit—quite common in nonfiction writing today—of trying to make the news more palatable by writing in a feature story style. Their leads consisted of a succession of tiny paragraphs that went something like this:

Whoosh!

It was incredible.

Something was definitely wrong.

Al Potter wondered if he was seeing things.

Or maybe it was just spring fever.

It wasn't as if he hadn't checked his car before leaving the house.

But then again, he hadn't remembered to tell Linda.

Which was odd, because he always remembered to tell Linda.

Ever since they started going together back in junior high.

And now there was also little Jo-Jo to worry about.

Come to think of it, the dog was acting kind of funny.

These articles often began on page 1, and I would read as far as the line that said "Continued on page 9" and still have no idea what they were about. Then I would dutifully turn to page 9 and find myself in an interesting story, full of unusual facts and detail. I'd say to the reporter, "That was a good story when I finally got to it—over here on page 9. Why didn't you put that stuff in your lead?" The reporter would say, "Well, in the lead I was writing color." The assumption is that fact and color are two separate entities. Of course they're not; color is organic to the fact. The writer's job is to present the colorful fact.

The problem, of course, is how to do this well, and there's one question that has to be asked right away: How strong a presence should the writer be in his presentation of the facts?

Until recently I felt that the writer should be involved in his story as much as possible. To write in the first person— "I," "we," "us"—is the warmest and most natural way of talking to another person on paper, which is what writing is. If the reader likes a writer's personality he will follow that writer anywhere.

In my own writing I have generally tried to make myself accessible. In this book, for instance, I want the reader to feel that he or she is hearing from someone who has wrestled with the craft of writing and is willing to share the experience. And that was the entire premise of my book *Writing with a Word Processor*. It was only secondarily an instruction manual. Primarily it was a personal journey into an alien technological land. I felt that most writers facing a word processor would have the same anxieties I did, and I wanted to make them identify with me, not with a mechanical process. Therefore the book begins with my first nervous visit to an IBM salesroom and ends with taking my disks to Harper & Row. But along the way there has been a whole psycho-drama of stress, frustration, humiliation, despair, anger, hope and, finally, romance. Readers of the book express their reaction with a fervor befitting a religious vision: "Thank you," they say, "for taking the fear out of the machine." So this is a personal approach that has always worked for me.

But my next book taught me—to my surprise—exactly the opposite lesson. I learned that a writer who intrudes on his material can hurt it badly. The book, *Willie and Dwike*, is a profile of two black jazz musicians, Willie Ruff and Dwike Mitchell, who have played together for thirty years as the Mitchell-Ruff Duo. Ruff plays the bass and the French horn; Mitchell is the pianist. I've known them since the early 1970s, when I was at Yale, where Ruff is a professor of music. Both men are superb musicians. But what gave me my affection for them was that teaching is a strong current in their lives. When they perform they usually avoid club dates, preferring to play at schools or colleges where they can explain jazz and give workshops. In 1959 they introduced jazz to the Soviet Union, playing and teaching for five weeks in Soviet conservatories. To reach those audiences Ruff taught himself Russian, which was his seventh language.

I wanted to know where they had acquired this teaching bent. Who had taught them—two poor boys growing up in isolated towns in the South? I started asking them about their boyhoods and found that their lives had been miraculously crossed, again and again, by someone who taught them what they needed to know next. I decided that I wanted to write a book about Mitchell and Ruff, which would really be a book about teaching and learning.

But before I started writing any of the boyhood material, Ruff told me that he and Mitchell were going to China to introduce jazz there. The Chinese had never heard live American jazz. Ruff had been taking intensive courses in Mandarin and felt that he was now fluent enough to make the trip. I said I'd like to go along and I asked *The New Yorker* if it would be interested in an article. The editor, William Shawn, said it sounded like a good story and I should aim for ten thousand words.

We flew to Shanghai and went to the Shanghai Conservatory of Music. There, Mitchell and Ruff gave a jazz concert for three hundred students and professors, who were crowded expectantly into a large room. As Ruff began to talk I could hardly contain my excitement over the antitheses that were at play around me. We were in the oldest conservatory in the oldest literate society in the world, where students pride themselves on being able to play a piece of music exactly the same way two hundred times, and they were listening to two black men, one of whom was speaking Chinese. And what he was explaining was an oral tradition that started in West Africa with drum language—a language so refined, Ruff said, that it could be used to tell stories and recite proverbs. "The drum is to West African society what the book is to literate society," he said. He could hardly have said anything more contrary to the culture of China.

Ruff explained how American jazz evolved out of that tradition, especially in its rhythms. But he said that jazz took its harmonic elements from the Protestant hymns that the slaves were encouraged to embrace, and to illustrate the point he and Mitchell played and sang a beautiful old Negro spiritual called "My Lord, What a Morning!" For me that was a painful moment. Being the only white American in the room, and knowing that Mitchell and Ruff were the great-grandsons of slaves, I heard a faraway sadness that none of the Chinese would have heard. It was an extra overlay of emotion on a situation that was emotional enough. Next, Ruff explained that the essence of jazz is improvisation. The Chinese don't even have a word for improvisation. Ruff translated it as "something created during the process of delivery."

Then Ruff began the concert. Near the end he and Mitchell played a meandering number that I had never heard before but that had an obvious shape: themes that had been stated earlier came back in different form. When it was over Ruff said, "We call that 'Shanghai Blues'—we just made it up." The Chinese found that unbelievable, and they began to pour out questions about improvisation, a mystery beyond their experience. Finally one professor said, "Do you really mean that you could improvise on any theme at all—one that you had never heard before?" Ruff said, "I would like to invite one of you to come up here and play a Chinese melody, and we will make a piece out of that."

The room erupted in oohs—the kind you hear at the circus—and a young Chinese man came forward and played a very Chinese piece on the piano. It was his own composition, about fourteen bars long—stately and beautiful and quite complex. Mitchell gave Ruff a look that said, "This time you've gone too far." But then he went to the piano and played the student's piece exactly—in the same key, and with the same chords, and with the same feeling. Then he began to embroider the piece, giving it a series of new lives but never violating its integrity, calling out the chord changes to Ruff on his bass. The Chinese were amazed by Mitchell's feat. They were also excited and moved, because they saw that for a jazz musician no point of departure is alien; even their own musical traditions could be embellished with beauty and respect. Music, finally, was the strongest force in the room. Despite the huge gulf between the two cultures—Chinese and black, written and oral, East and West—the gap was closed.

I went back to New York and wrote my ten thousand words and sent them to *The New Yorker*. The piece began and ended with the concert and it had two flashbacks—one that explained who Mitchell and Ruff were and how I happened to know them, and one that described the conservatory and the traumatic effect of the Cultural Revolution that had closed it for ten years and jailed all its professors. Shawn called to say that he liked the piece but that he would want to cut all the parts in which I expressed an opinion about Mitchell and Ruff and their music. I thought, "That kills it—surely the reader needs to know about my emotional involvement with these men and why I admire them so much as artists and as teachers." But my second thought was to trust Shawn's judgment. So the piece was duly edited. None of my words were changed, but every sentence or phrase was removed that put an interpretation on a fact. I remained in the piece as a reporter, but not as a person.

When the article was published it had more emotional impact than anything I had ever written. This was a revelation to me. People said to my wife, "Bill really knows those two men very well, doesn't he?" That was also mysterious: how did they know? Finally I realized that the material itself was so rich that any attempt to explain it would be patronizing. It would take away from the reader the pleasure of making his own connections, of bringing his own emotions to whatever parts of the story happened to touch some corner of his life. In fact, many readers of my article made connections that had never occurred to me. I understood—perhaps for the first time—that the reader plays a major role in the act of writing and must be given room to play it.

The Shanghai piece became the first chapter of my book *Willie and Dwike*. Then I went back to the beginning and wrote the rest of it: one chapter about Mitchell's boyhood in Florida and one about Ruff's boyhood in Alabama; a chapter about the army base in Ohio where the two men met and were taught by a group of brilliant black musicians; a chapter about a week they spent in the Quad Cities of Iowa and Illinois giving concerts and workshops in schools and colleges; a chapter about Mitchell as a teacher and a pianist, and a final chapter about a trip Ruff made to Venice to play Gregorian chants on the French horn in St. Mark's basilica, alone at night, to record its astonishing acoustics. (I also went along on these trips.) Throughout, I doggedly applied the Shawn principle, trusting my material and trying never to explain it. It's very American material, full of surprising teachers and small triumphs over the odds of being born black in America in the 1930s, and I began to take pleasure in it as material and in the task of organizing it: imposing a shape on it and presenting it clearly.

When I finished the manuscript I sent it to three of my former students at Yale—now good writers and editors themselves—and asked them to look for any sentence or word that told the reader something he had already been told, or that he was about to be told, or that was implicit, or that was gratuitous in any way. Between them they found about two dozen specimens, and I cut them all gratefully, getting the manuscript down to the bone. I don't think it even has any adverbs, like "predictably" or "surprisingly," that put a value on a fact before the reader encounters the fact. The result is a book that readers almost unanimously call moving. But what makes it moving is its content. The facts generate their own emotions.

I've described this experience because I hope it will help other writers as much as it helped me. It has also sharpened my awareness of how much writers say that doesn't need to be said—and how annoying this is to the reader. Today I find that I stop reading many articles and books because the writer keeps telling me something he has already told me or enabled me to surmise, or he keeps asking rhetorical questions that both he and I have already answered. What a writer least wants to do is make a reader stop reading, and one of the quickest ways is to irritate him.

In urging you to trust your material I don't mean that keeping yourself out of your article is the only way to write. Different subjects call for different approaches. Your task as a writer is to present your material in the way that serves it best: to find the right voice for it, and the right language, and the right shape. Maybe you should be strongly present in your story; maybe not—usually the material tells us at the start how it wants to be written. But after that the writer must be in charge.

Therefore learn to take as much pride in organizing your article as you do in writing it. It's a more subtle skill than writing elegant individual sentences and is often neglected. But all your elegant sentences will add up to chaos if you don't remember that writing is linear and sequential, that logic is the glue that holds it together, that tension and pace are crucial. Every component in a piece of writing must do new work, and the transitions must pull the reader from one sentence to the next without his noticing the tug. This is where the game is ultimately won or lost: in the hundreds of small details that tell the reader, if only subconsciously, that he's in the hands of a careful writer.

Trust your material—it's stronger than you think. But it's only as strong as the structure you build for it and the control you maintain over it from the first sentence to the last.

22. Write as Well as You Can

I'm occasionally asked if I can recall the moment when I knew I wanted to be a writer. No such blinding flash occurred. But I can point to a set of attitudes that I inherited early in life and that have guided me ever since. They came from both sides of my family, by totally different routes.

My mother loved good writing, and she found it as often in newspapers as she did in books. She regularly clipped columns and articles out of the paper that delighted her with their graceful use of language, or their wit, or their original vision of life. Because of her I knew at an early age that good writing can appear anywhere, even in the lowly newspaper, and that what matters is the writing itself, not the medium in which it is published. Therefore I've always tried to write as well as I could by my own standards; I've never changed my style to fit the size or the presumed education of the audience I was writing for. My mother was also a person of tremendous humor and optimism. These are lubricants in writing, as they are in life, and a writer lucky enough to have them in his baggage will start the day with an extra round of confidence.

Originally I wasn't meant to be a writer. My father was a businessman. His grandfather had come from Germany in the immigration of 1849 with a formula for making shellac. He built a small house and factory in a rocky field far uptown in Manhattan—at what is now Fifty-ninth Street and Tenth

Avenue—and started a business called William Zinsser & Company. I still have a photograph of that pastoral scene; the land slopes down toward the Hudson River, and the only living creature is a goat. The firm stayed at that location until 1973, when it moved to New Jersey.

For a business to remain in the same family on the same Manhattan block for more than a century is rare, and as a boy I couldn't escape the naggings of continuity, for I was the fourth William Zinsser and the only son; my father's fate was to have three daughters first. He was a man who loved his business. When he talked about it I never felt that he regarded it as a venture for making money, but as an art, to be practiced with imagination and only the best materials. He had a passion for quality and had no patience with the second-rate. As far as I know, he never went into a store looking for a bargain. He charged more for his product because he made it with the best ingredients, and his company prospered. It was a ready-made future for me, and my father looked forward to the day when I would join him.

But inevitably a different day arrived. I always knew in my heart that I wanted to be a newspaperman, and not long after I came home from the army I got a job on the *New York Herald Tribune* and had to tell my father that I wasn't going to carry on the family business. He accepted the news with his usual generosity and wished me well in my chosen field. I couldn't have received a finer gift. I was liberated from having to fulfill somebody else's expectations, which were not the right ones for me. I was free to succeed or fail on my own terms.

Only later did I realize that I took along on my journey another gift from my father: a bone-deep belief that quality is its own reward. I, too, have never gone into a store looking for a bargain. Ironically, though my mother was the literary one in our family—the magpie collector of books, the ardent lover of the English language, the writer of dazzling letters—it was from the world of business that I absorbed my craftsman's ethic, and over the years, when I found myself endlessly rewriting what I had endlessly rewritten, determined to write better than everybody else who was competing for the same space, the inner voice that I was hearing was the voice of my father talking about shellac.

Besides wanting to write as well as possible, I wanted to write as entertainingly as possible. When I tell aspiring writers that they should think of themselves as part entertainer, they don't like to hear it—the word smacks of carnivals and jugglers and clowns. But to succeed you must make your piece jump out of a newspaper or a magazine by being more diverting than everyone else's piece. You must find some way to elevate your act of writing into an entertainment. Usually this means giving the reader an enjoyable surprise. Any number of methods will do the job: humor, anecdote, paradox, an unexpected quotation, a powerful fact, an outlandish detail, a circuitous approach, an elegant arrangement of words. These seeming amusements in fact become your "style." When we say that we like a writer's style, what we really mean is that we like his personality as he expresses it on paper. Given a choice between two traveling companions—and a writer is someone who asks us to travel with him—we will choose the one who makes an effort to brighten the trip.

Unlike medicine or the other sciences, writing has no new discoveries to spring on us. We're in no danger of reading in our morning newspaper that a breakthrough has been made in how to write a clear English sentence—that information has been around since the King James Bible. We know, for instance, that verbs have more vigor than nouns, that active verbs are better than passive verbs, that short words and sentences are easier to read than long ones, that concrete details are easier to picture than vague abstractions.

Obviously the rules have often been bent. Victorian writers had a taste for the ornate and didn't consider brevity a virtue, and many modern writers—like Tom Wolfe and Norman Mailer today—have broken out of the cage, turning a headlong exuberance of language into a source of positive energy. Such skillful acrobats, however, are rare; most nonfiction writers will do well to cling to the ropes of simplicity and clarity. We may be given new technologies like the word processor to ease the burdens of composition. But on the whole we know what we need to know. We are all working with the same words and principles.

Where, then, is the edge? Ninety percent of the answer lies in the hard work of mastering the tools discussed in earlier chapters of this book. Add a few percentage points for such natural gifts as a good ear, a sense of rhythm and a feeling for words. But the final advantage is the same one that applies in every other competitive venture. If you would like to write better than everybody else, you have to *want* to write better than everybody else. You must take an obsessive pride in the smallest details of your craft. And you must be willing to defend what you've written against the various middlemen—editors, agents and publishers—whose sights may be different from yours, or whose standards may not be as high. Too many writers are browbeaten into settling for less than their best.

I've always felt that my "style"—the careful projection onto paper of who I think I am—was my only marketable asset, the only possession that might set me apart from other writers. Therefore I've never wanted anyone to fiddle with it, and after I submit an article I protect it fiercely. Several magazine editors have told me that I'm the only writer they know who cares what happens to his piece after he gets paid for it. Most writers won't argue with an editor because they don't want to annoy him; they're so grateful to be published that they agree to having their style—in other words, their personality—violated in public.

But to defend what you've written is a sign that you are alive. I'm a known crank on this issue—I fight over every semicolon—but editors put up with me because they see that I'm serious. In fact, my crankiness has brought me far more work than it has driven away. Editors with an unusual assignment often thought of me because they knew I would do it with unusual care. They also knew, incidentally, that they would get it on time and that it would be accurate. Remember that the craft of nonfiction writing involves more than writing; it also means being reliable. Editors will properly drop a writer they can't count on.

Which brings us to editors. Are they friends or enemies—gods who save us from our sins or bums who trample on our poetic souls? Like the rest of creation, they come in all varieties. I think with gratitude of a half-dozen editors who sharpened my writing by changing its focus or its emphasis, or detecting weaknesses of logic or structure, or suggesting a different lead, or letting me talk a problem through with them when I couldn't decide between several possible routes, or cutting various forms of excess. Twice I threw out an entire chapter of a book because an editor told me it was unnecessary—and both of them were right. But above all I remember those editors for their generosity. They had an enthusiasm for whatever project we were trying to bring off together as writer and editor. Their confidence that I could make it work often kept me going.

What a good editor brings to a piece of writing is an objective eye that the writer has long since lost, and there is no end of ways in which an editor can improve a manuscript: pruning, shaping, clarifying, tidying a hundred inconsistencies of tense and pronoun and location and tone, noticing all the sentences that could be read in two different ways, dividing awkward long sentences into short ones, putting the writer back on the main road if he has strayed down a side path, building bridges where the writer has lost the reader by not paying attention to his transitions. An editor's hand must also be invisible. Whatever he adds in his own words shouldn't sound like his own words; they should sound like the writer's words.

For all these acts of salvation, editors can't be thanked fervently enough. Unfortunately, they can also do considerable harm. In general the damage takes two forms: altering style and altering content. Let's look at style first.

A good editor likes nothing better than a piece of copy that he hardly has to touch. A bad editor has a compulsion to tinker, proving with busywork that he hasn't forgotten the minutiae of grammar and usage. He is a literal fellow, catching cracks in the road but not enjoying the scenery. Very often it simply doesn't occur to him that a writer is writing by ear, trying to achieve a particular sound or cadence, or playing with words just for the pleasures of wordplay. One of the bleakest moments for a writer is the one when he realizes that the editor has missed the point of what he is trying to do.

I remember many such dismal revelations. A minor one that comes to mind involved an article I wrote about a program called "Visiting Artists" that brought artists and musicians to a group of Midwestern cities that were economically depressed. Describing them, I wrote: "They don't look like cities that get visited by many visiting artists." When the galleys came back the sentence said: "They don't look like cities that are on the itinerary of many visiting artists." A small point? Not to me. I had used repetition because it's a device I like—it takes the reader by surprise and refreshes him in mid-sentence. But the editor remembered the rule about substituting synonyms for words that are repeated, and he corrected my error. When I called to protest, he was amazed. We argued for a long time, neither of us yielding. Finally he said, "You really feel strongly about this, don't you?" I feel strongly that one such erosion leads to another and that the writer must take a stand. I've even bought articles back from magazines that made changes that I wouldn't accept. If you allow your distinctiveness to be edited out you will lose one of your main advantages.

Ideally the relationship between a writer and an editor should be one of negotiation and trust. Frequently, for instance, an editor will make a change to clarify a muddy sentence and will inadvertently lose an important point—a fact or a nuance that the writer included for reasons that the editor didn't know about. In such cases the writer should ask to have his point back. The editor, if he agrees, should oblige. But he should also insist on his right to fix whatever had been unclear. Clarity is what every editor owes the reader. An editor should never allow something in print that he doesn't understand himself. If he doesn't understand it, at least one other person won't understand it, and that's one too many. The process, in short, is one in which the writer and the editor proceed through the manuscript together, finding for every problem the solution that best serves the finished article.

It's a process, incidentally, that can be done just as well over the phone as in person. Don't let editors use distance or their own disarray as an excuse for altering your work without your consent. "We were on deadline," "we were already late," "the person who usually deals with you was out sick," "we had a big shake-up here last week"—these dreary phrases cloak a multitude of inefficiencies and sins. One startling change in the publishing profession has been the steady erosion of courtesies that were once routine. Magazine editors, especially, have become cavalier about a whole series of actions that should be automatic: notifying the writer that the piece has arrived, reading it with reasonable speed, telling the writer whether it's O.K., returning it immediately if it's not, working supportively with the writer if the piece needs changes, sending the writer galley proofs, seeing that the writer gets paid promptly. Writers are vulnerable enough without being put through the repeated indignities of writing or calling to learn the status of their article and to beg for their money. The prevailing notion seems to be that "courtesies" are merely frills and can therefore be forgotten. On the contrary, they are organic to the craft. They are the code of honor that anchors the whole enterprise, and editors who forget them are toying with nothing less than the writer's fundamental rights.

This arrogance is at its most injurious when an editor goes beyond changes of style or structure and enters the sacred realm of content. I often hear free-lance writers say something like this: "When I got the magazine I looked for my article and I didn't even recognize it. They had written a whole new lead and had me saying a lot of other things that aren't what I believe at all."

That's the cardinal sin—tampering with a writer's opinions. But editors will do what writers let them do, especially if time is short. Writers acquiesce in their own humiliation. With every surrender they remind editors that they can be treated like hired help. In part this treatment grows out of another new trend in publishing: the rise of the special-interest magazine. Not long ago America had many magazines that took the whole world as their domain, like the old *Life* and *Saturday Evening Post,* and their writers were generalists who brought individuality to their articles. Today there are far more magazines, but their world has shrunk. Most of them have been created to provide information about one specialized field. In fact, no field would seem to be too specialized—if your interest is personal computers that can do spreadsheets in Arabic, there's a magazine for you. The result is a nation of magazines that are being edited by formula. The editors feel secure with their formula and don't want any deviation. A writer who tries a fresh approach will usually find his piece rewritten by the editors to serve their own purposes.

But finally the purposes that a writer serves must be his own. What you write is yours and nobody else's. Take your talent as far as you can and guard it with your life. Only you know how far that is; no editor knows. Writing well means believing in your writing and believing in yourself, taking risks, daring to be different, pushing yourself to excel. You will only write as well as you make yourself write.

My favorite definition of a careful writer comes from Joe DiMaggio, though he didn't know that that's what he was defining. DiMaggio was the greatest player I ever saw, and nobody looked more relaxed. He covered vast distances in the outfield, moving in graceful strides, always arriving ahead of the ball, making the hardest catch look routine, and even when he was at bat, hitting the ball with tremendous power, he didn't appear to be exerting himself. I marveled at how effortless he looked because what he did could only be achieved by great effort. A reporter once asked him about this, and he said: "I always thought that there was at least one person in the stands who had never seen me play, and I didn't want to let him down."

Sources

Most of the material by other writers that I have quoted in these pages was first written for a magazine or a newspaper and was subsequently reprinted in a book. In general the source cited below is for the original hardcover edition of the book. Many of these editions are now out of print but are available in public libraries. In many other cases the book has been reprinted in paperback and is relatively easy to obtain.

P 28–29. Preface by E. B. White to *A Basic Chicken Guide* by Roy E. Jones. Copyright 1944 by Roy E. Jones. Reprinted by permission of William Morrow & Co. Also appears in *The Second Tree from the Corner*. Harper & Bros., 1954.

P 29–30. "The Hills of Zion," by H. L. Mencken, from *The Vintage Mencken*, gathered by Alistair Cooke. Vintage Books (paper), 1955.

P 31–33. *How to Survive in Your Native Land*, by James Herndon. Simon & Schuster, 1971. Reprinted by permission of Simon & Schuster, a Division of Gulf & Western Corporation.

P 66–70. *The Lunacy Boom*, by William Zinsser. Harper & Row, 1970.

P 72. *Slouching Towards Bethlehem*, by Joan Didion. Farrar, Straus & Giroux, 1968, Copyright © 1966 by Joan Didion. Reprinted by permission of the publisher.

P 74. "Court Buff," by Mark Singer. From *The New Yorker*, Dec. 15, 1980. Reprinted by permission. © 1980 Mark Singer.

P 67. *Nixon Agonistes*, by Garry Wills. Houghton Mifflin, 1970. Reprinted by permission of the publisher.

P 69. "The Last Time I Played Rugby," by Richard Burton. From *The Observer* (London), Oct. 4, 1970.

P 79. *Nixon Agonistes*.

P 80. "Coolidge," by H. L. Mencken, from *The Vintage Mencken*.

P 80–81. *Pop Goes America*.

P 93–95. *The Bottom of the Harbor*, by Joseph Mitchell. Little, Brown and Company, 1960. Reprinted by permission of Harold Ober Associates, Incorporated. © 1960 by Joseph Mitchell.

P 99–100. *Slouching Towards Bethlehem*.

P 101–2. *Coming into the Country*, by John McPhee. Farrar, Straus and Giroux, 1977.

P 102–3. *A Walker in the City*, by Alfred Kazin. Harcourt, Brace, 1951.

P 104–5. *No Room in the Ark*, by Alan Moorehead. Reprinted by permission of Harper & Row, Publishers, Inc.

P 106–7. *The Offensive Traveller*, by V. S. Pritchett. Alfred A. Knopf, 1964.

P 108–9. *Of a Fire on the Moon*, by Norman Mailer. Little, Brown and Company, 1971. © 1969, 1970 by Norman Mailer. By permission of the publisher.

P 135–37. "Brain Signals in Test Foretell Action," Feb. 13, 1971, by Harold M. Schmeck, Jr. © 1971 by the New York Times Company. Reprinted by permission.

P 137–38. "The Mystery of Memory," by Will Bradbury. *Life*, Nov. 12, 1971. ©
1971, Time Inc. Reprinted with permission.

P 139. *Eleven Blue Men and Other Narratives of Medical Detection*, by Berton
Roueché. Little, Brown and Company, 1954.

P 140–41. *Beyond Habitat*, by Moshe Safdie. The M.I.T. Press, 1970.

P 141–42. *The Immense Journey*, by Loren Eiseley. Random House, 1957.

P 142–43. *The Lives of a Cell: Notes of a Biology Watcher*, by Lewis Thomas.
Viking Press, 1974.

P 144. *Weapons and Hope*, by Freeman Dyson. Harper & Row, 1983.

P 162. "Hub Fans Bid Kid Adieu," by John Updike. From *Assorted Prose*, by John
Updike. Alfred A. Knopf, 1965.

P 164. *Late Innings*, by Roger Angell. Simon & Schuster, 1982.

P 166. *Life on the Run*, by Bill Bradley. Quadrangle/The New York Times Book
Co., 1976.

P 167. "In Indiana, The Roar of the Motor Is the Sweetest Sound," May 26, 1974,
by Jean Shepherd. © 1974 by the New York Times Company. Reprinted by
permission.

P 173–74. *Agee on Film*, by James Agee. McDowell Obolensky, 1958.

P 174–75. *Living-Room War*, by Michael J. Arlen. Viking Press, 1969.

P 176–77. *The Musical Scene*, by Virgil Thomson. Alfred A. Knopf, 1945.

P 177–78. "On Writing Operas and Staging Them," by Virgil Thomson. *Parnassus:
Poetry in Review*, vol. 10, no. 2 (Fall/Winter 1982).

P 179–80. "Virginia Woolf," Nov. 5, 1972, by Michael Rosenthal. © 1972 by the
New York Times Company. Reprinted by permission.

P 185–86. *The Haircurl Papers*, by William Zinsser. Harper & Row, 1964.

P 191–92. *The America of George Ade*, edited, with an introduction by Jean Shepherd. G. P. Putnam's Sons, 1961.

P 193–94. *Shut Up, He Explained*, a Ring Lardner Selection. Charles Scribner's
Sons, 1962.

P 194–95. *Archy and Mehitabel*, by Don Marquis. Doubleday & Co., 1927.

P 195–96. *The Owl in the Attic and Other Perplexities*, by James Thurber. Harper
& Bros., 1931.

P 196. *The Crazy Fool*, by Donald Ogden Stewart. Albert & Charles Boni, 1925.

P 196–97. *Benchley—or Else!*, by Robert C. Benchley. Harper & Bros., 1947.

P 193–99. *Strictly from Hunger*, by S. J. Perelman. Random House, 1937. Also in
The Most of S. J. Perelman, Simon & Schuster, 1958.

P 199–200. *Getting Even*, by Woody Allen. Random House, 1971.

Note: Portions of Chapter 7 and Chapter 16 first appeared in *Life* and *The New
York Times Magazine*, respectively.

Index